# BERKHAMSTED IN 50 BUILDINGS

## PAUL RABBITTS AND PETER JEFFREE

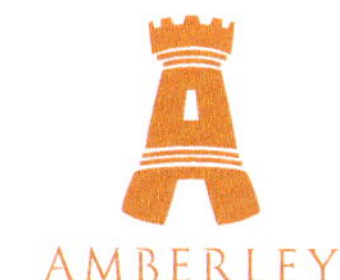

AMBERLEY

First published 2026

Amberley Publishing, The Hill, Stroud
Gloucestershire GL5 4EP

www.amberley-books.com



British Library Cataloguing in Publication Data.
A catalogue record for this book is available from the British Library.

ISBN 978 1 3981 2838 5 (print)
ISBN 978 1 3981 2839 2 (ebook)

Typesetting by SJmagic DESIGN SERVICES, India.
Printed in Great Britain.

Appointed GPSR EU Representative:
Easy Access System Europe Oü, 16879218
Address: Mustamäe tee 50, 10621, Tallinn, Estonia
Contact Details: gpsr.requests@easproject.com, +358 40 500 3575

# Contents

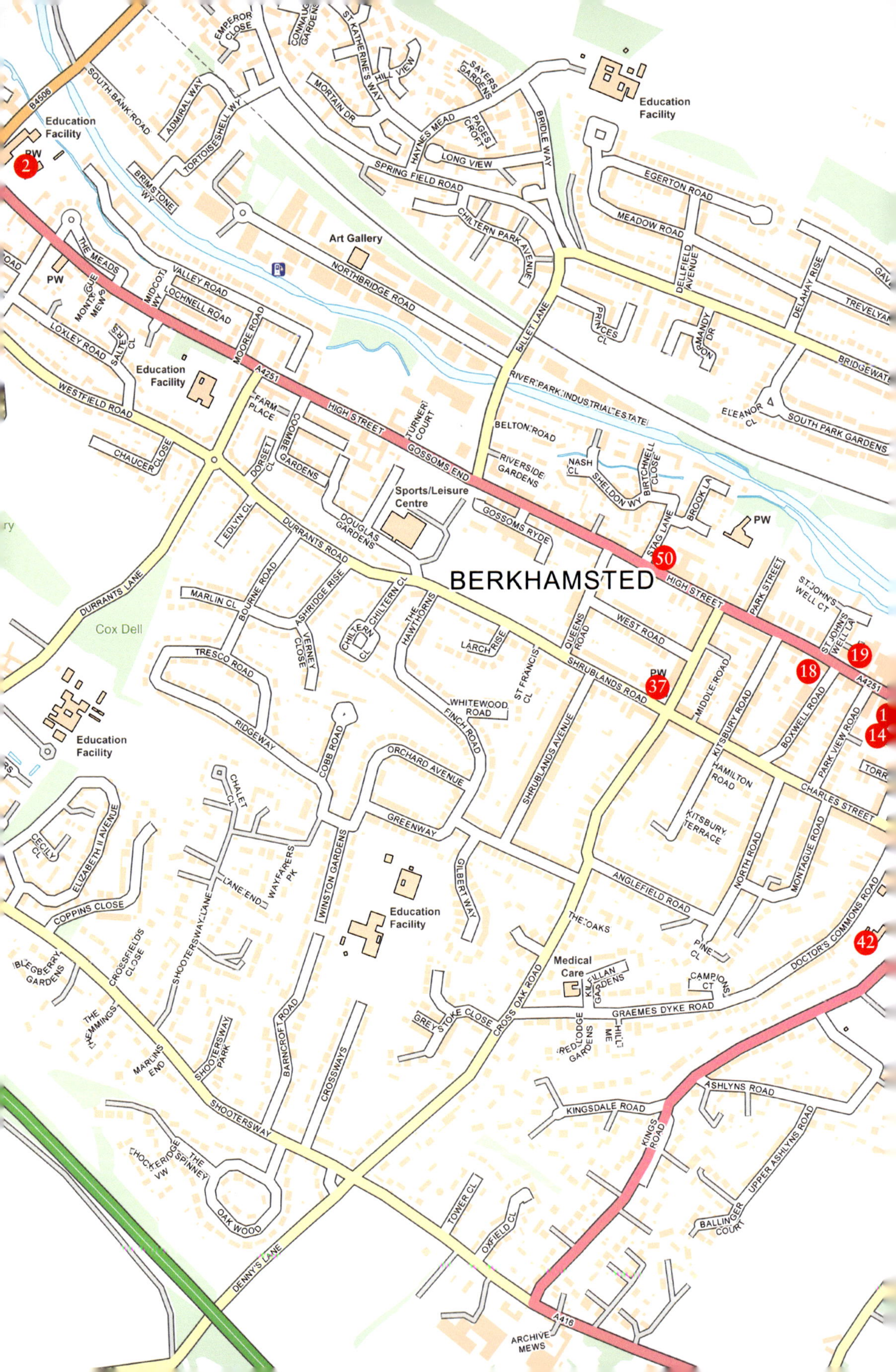
BERKHAMSTED
Education Facility
Education Facility
Education Facility
Education Facility
Art Gallery
Sports/Leisure Centre
Medical Care
PW
PW
PW
PW
B4506
SOUTH BANK ROAD
ADMIRAL WAY
EMPEROR CLOSE
CONNAUGHT GARDENS
ST KATHERINE'S WAY
HILL VIEW
MORTAIN DR
SAYERS GARDENS
PAGES CROFT
BRIDLE WAY
HAYNES MEAD
LONG VIEW
SPRING FIELD ROAD
CHILTERN PARK AVENUE
EGERTON ROAD
MEADOW ROAD
DELLFIELD AVENUE
DELAHAY RISE
TREVELYAN
GAV
BRIDGEWATER
MANDY DR
TORTOISESHELL WY
BRIMSTONE WY
THE MEADS
MONTAGUE MEWS
SALTERS CL
LOXLEY ROAD
WESTFIELD ROAD
PW
VALLEY ROAD
MIDCOT WY
LOCHNELL ROAD
MOORE ROAD
A4251
FARM PLACE
DORSET CL
COOMBE GARDENS
HIGH STREET
GOSSOMS END
TURNER COURT
BELTON ROAD
RIVERSIDE GARDENS
RIVER PARK INDUSTRIAL ESTATE
NASH CL
SHELDON WY
BIRTCHNELL CLOSE
BROOK LA
STAG LANE
PRINCES CL
BILLET LANE
CHILTERN PARK AVENUE
NORTHBRIDGE ROAD
CHAUCER CLOSE
EDUCATION FACILITY
DURRANTS LANE
Cox Dell
MARLIN CL
BOURNE ROAD
EDLYN CL
DURRANTS ROAD
ASHRIDGE RISE
DOUGLAS GARDENS
CHILTERN CL
CHILTERN CL
VERNEY CLOSE
THE HAWTHORNS
GOSSOMS RYDE
WEST ROAD
QUEENS ROAD
SHRUBLANDS ROAD
HIGH STREET
PARK STREET
ST JOHN'S WELL CT
ST JOHN'S WELL LA
A4251
TRESCO ROAD
LARCH RISE
ST FRANCIS CL
MIDDLE ROAD
KITSBURY ROAD
BOXWELL ROAD
PARK VIEW ROAD
TORR
Education Facility
ELIZABETH II AVENUE
CECILY CL
RIDGEWAY
CHALET CL
LANE END
WAYFARERS PK
WINSTON GARDENS
COBB ROAD
ORCHARD AVENUE
WHITEWOOD ROAD
FINCH ROAD
SHRUBLANDS AVENUE
GREENWAY
GILBERT WAY
HAMILTON ROAD
KITSBURY TERRACE
NORTH ROAD
MONTAGUE ROAD
CHARLES STREET
ANGLEFIELD ROAD
PINE CL
CAMPIONS CT
DOCTOR'S COMMONS ROAD
COPPINS CLOSE
CROSSFIELDS CLOSE
SHOOTERSWAY LANE
SHOOTERSWAY PARK
BARNCROFT ROAD
CROSSWAYS
GREYSTOKE CLOSE
CROSS OAK ROAD
THE OAKS
Medical Care
KILLILAN GARDENS
GRAEMES DYKE ROAD
RED LODGE GARDENS
HILL ME
BLEGBERRY GARDENS
THE HEMMINGS
MARLINS END
SHOOTERSWAY
HOCKERIDGE VW
THE SPINNEY
OAK WOOD
DENNY'S LANE
TOWER CL
OXFIELD CL
KINGSDALE ROAD
KINGS ROAD
ASHLYNS ROAD
BALLINGER COURT
UPPER ASHLYNS ROAD
ARCHIVE MEWS
A416
ELEANOR CL
SOUTH PARK GARDENS

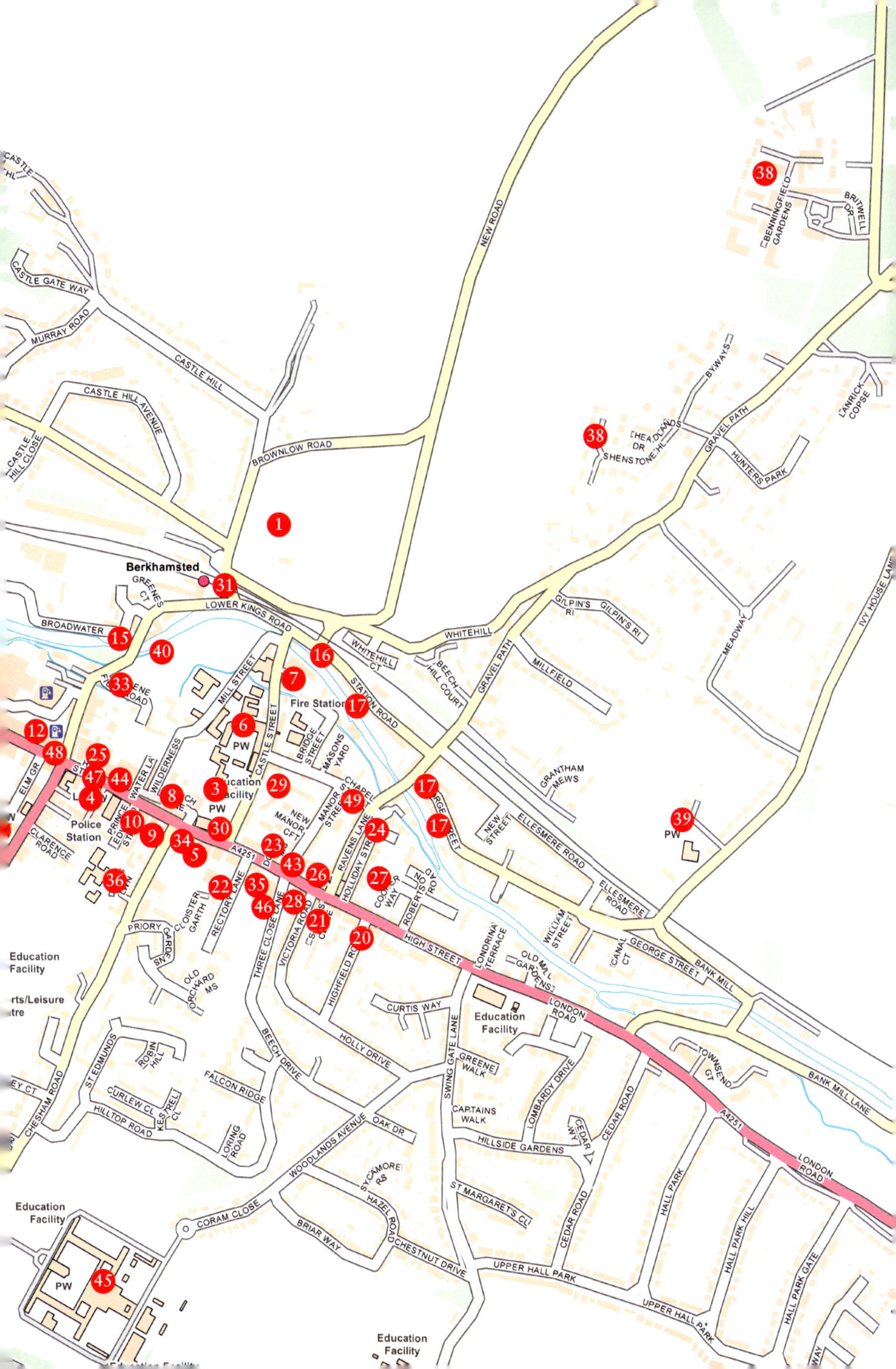

Berkhamsted
CASTLE HL
CASTLE GATE WAY
MURRAY ROAD
CASTLE HILL
CASTLE HILL AVENUE
CASTLE HILL CLOSE
BROWNLOW ROAD
NEW ROAD
BENNINGFIELD GARDENS
BRITWELL DR
L'ANRICK COPSE
HEADLANDS DR
SHENSTONE HL
BYWAYS
GRAVEL PATH
HUNTERS PARK
IVY HOUSE LANE
GREENES CT
LOWER KINGS ROAD
GILPIN'S RI
GILPIN'S RI
WHITEHILL
MEADWAY
BROADWATER
WHITEHILL CT
BEECH HILL COURT
GRAVEL PATH
MILLFIELD
GREENE ROAD
MILL STREET
FIRE STATION
BRIDGE STREET
CASTLE STREET
MASONS YARD
STATION ROAD
WHITEHILL
GRANTHAM MEWS
Education Facility
ELM GR
PW
WILDERNESS
WATER LA
CHAPEL
MANOR STREET
RAVENS LANE
HOLLIDAY STR
GEORGE STREET
NEW STREET
ELLESMERE ROAD
PW
Police Station
PRINCES EDWARD ST
NEW MANOR CFT
DEAN
ROBERTS RD
COOPER WAY
ROBERTS RO
WILLIAM STREET
ELLESMERE ROAD
CANAL
GEORGE STREET
BANK MILL
CLARENCE ROAD
A4251
RECTORY LANE
THREE CLOSE LANE
VICTORIA ROAD
HIGHFIELD RD
HIGH STREET
LONDRINA TERRACE
OLD MILL GARDENS
George Street
BANK MILL LANE
PRIORY GARDENS
CLOISTER GARTH
OLD ORCHARD MS
BEECH DRIVE
CURTIS WAY
SWING GATE LANE
GREENE WALK
Education Facility
LONDON ROAD
A4251
LONDON ROAD
Education Facility
ST EDMUNDS ROAD
CHESHAM ROAD
ROBIN HILL
CURLEW CL
KESTREL CL
HILLTOP ROAD
FALCON RIDGE
LORING ROAD
WOODLANDS AVENUE
OAK DR
SYCAMORE RS
HAZEL ROAD
CHESTNUT DRIVE
CORAM CLOSE
BRIAR WAY
CAPTAINS WALK
LOMBARDY DRIVE
HILLSIDE GARDENS
CEDAR WY
CEDAR ROAD
ST MARGARET'S CLI
HALL PARK
TOWNSEND GT
HALL PARK HILL
UPPER HALL PARK
HALL PARK GATE
UPPER HALL PARK
LONDON ROAD
Education Facility
Education Facility
Arts/Leisure Centre
PW

# Key

1. Berkhamsted Castle and Cottage
2. St Mary's Church and Almshouses, Northchurch
3. St Peter's Church
4. No. 173 High Street
5. Dean Incent's House
6. Berkhamsted School
7. The Boote
8. Court House
9. The Swan Inn
10. The Kings Arms
11. Sayer's Almshouse
12. Former William Cowper's School
13. The Former Bourne School
14. The George Inn
15. Lock-keepers Cottage, Grand Union Canal
16. Port of Berkhamsted
17. The Rising Sun/The Boat/The Crystal Palace
18. Quaker Meeting House
19. James Wood & Son
20. The Pightle House
21. The Poplars
22. The Red House
23. The Dower House
24. Brownlow House
25. Berkhamsted Town Hall
26. Sibdon Place
27. Berkhamsted Baptist Church
28. The Goat Public House
29. Former Gardener's Arms
30. Admiral House
31. Berkhamsted Railway Station
32. Kings Road Churches
33. A. C. Meeks Livery and Hunting Stables
34. Overton House
35. Clementine Churchill's Home, No. 107 High Street
36. Graham Greene's Birthplace
37. All Saints' Church
38. The Mansion
39. Sunnyside Church
40. Castle Mill
41. H. H. Dickman, Chemist
42. The Beeches
43. No. 90 High Street
44. Home and Colonial
45. Ashlyns School
46. The Rex and the Gatsby
47. Berkhamsted Civic Centre
48. Former DeLisle Jewellers
49. Site of Former Counting House
50. Modern Berkhamsted

# Introduction

In March 2010, Dacorum Borough Council commissioned a character appraisal for the town centre of Berkhamsted. Many of the buildings within this book fall within this part of the town. The report describes the historical development of Berkhamsted as being influenced by the natural valley landscape and the River Bulbourne, together with the impact of human development by way of Berkhamsted Castle, the Grand Union Canal and the railway line.

The plan of Berkhamsted town centre is typical of a medieval market settlement; the linear High Street forms the spine of the town from which extend medieval

Nos 74–104 High Street, part of the spine of the town.

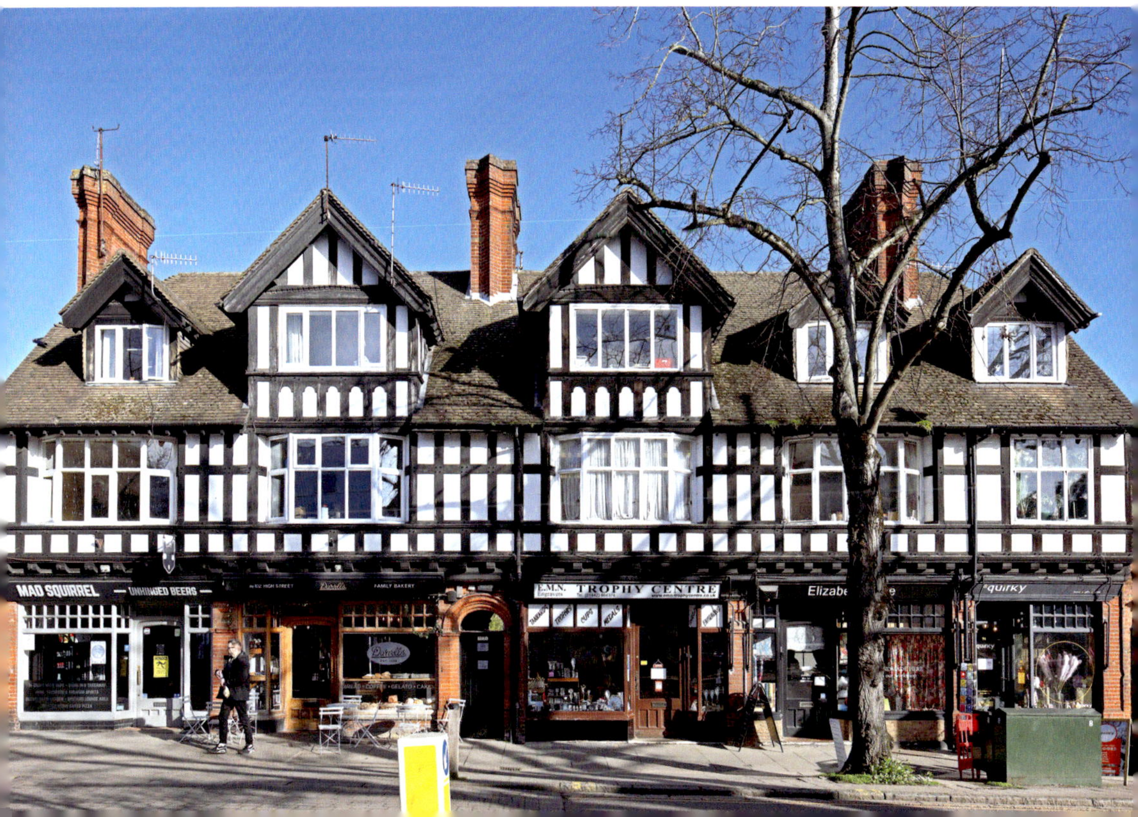

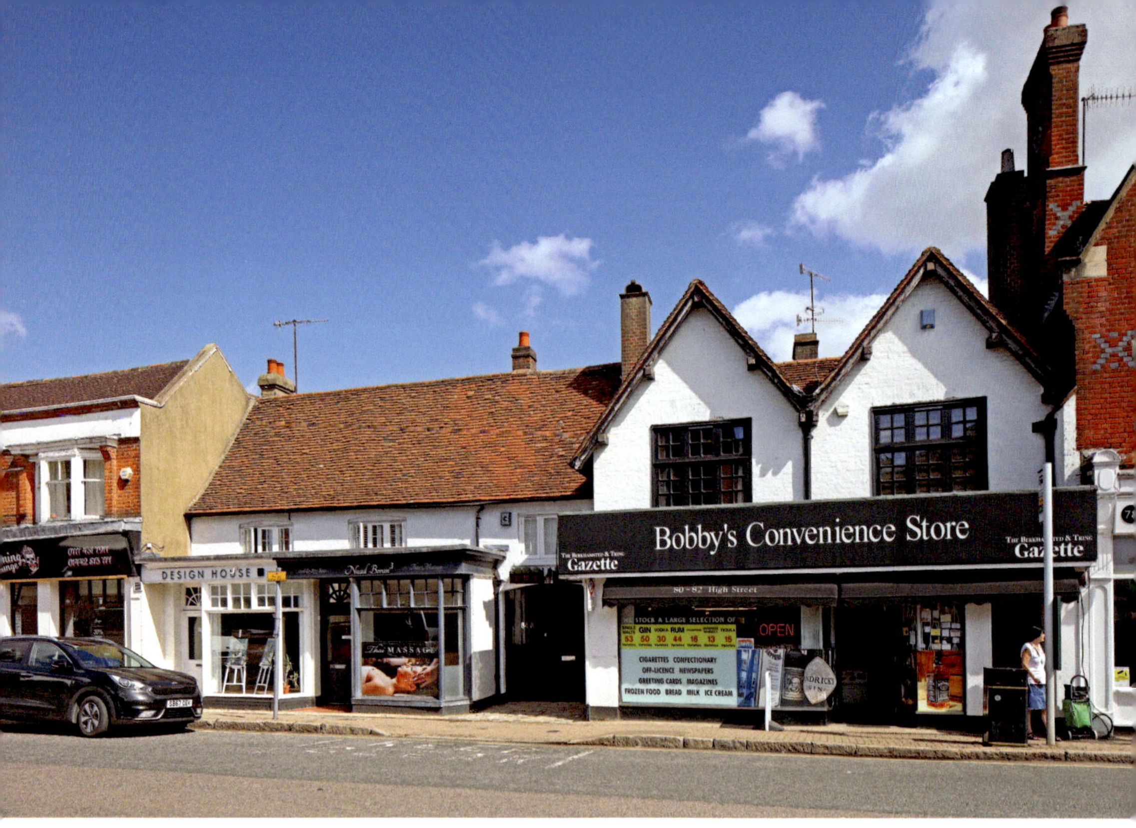

Nos 74–104 High Street.

burgage plots. At the centre stands the beautiful parish church (the thirteenth-century Church of St Peter) along with the triangular marketplace (the old Market Place, recorded as 'Le Shopperowe' in 1357). The majority of the buildings along the High Street date to between the sixteenth and nineteenth centuries and are mostly commercial premises (such as shops, restaurants, banks, offices, public houses), places of worship and public buildings with a smaller number of residential properties.

Later streets were laid out on the valley sides away from the High Street according to need (a growing population), and were influenced by the existing plots/field systems and the landscape topography. These streets were mainly built during the nineteenth century and predominantly lay to the southwest of the High Street, with some lying close to the areas occupied by the Grand Union Canal and the railway line. The result is an eclectic mix of architecture, with fifty of them chosen for the subject of this book. It also concludes with a number of newer, more modern buildings that have become part of the town's architecture, emphasising the changing needs and demands of a growing population, but also the challenges faced by planners and architects in ensuring suitability, style and at the same time displaying new fashions in architecture.

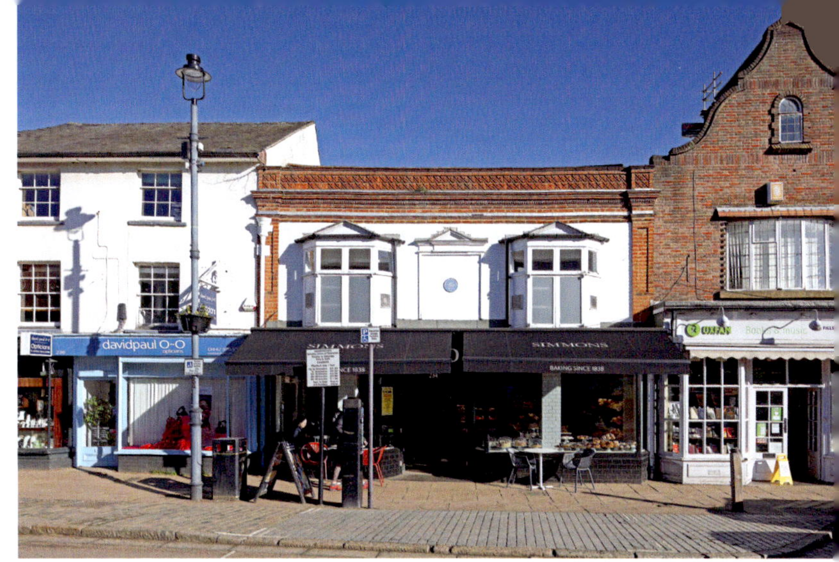

No. 234 High Street, an eclectic mix of architecture.

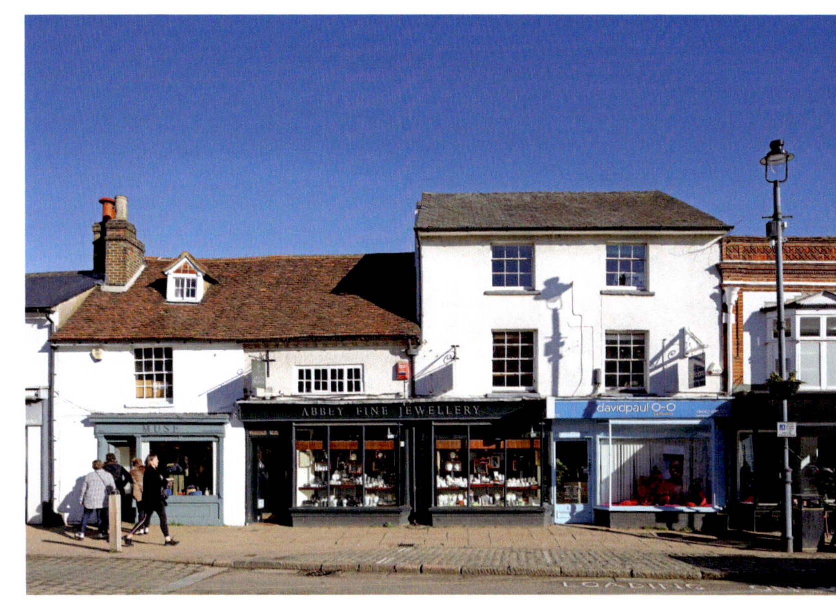

No. 238 High Street.

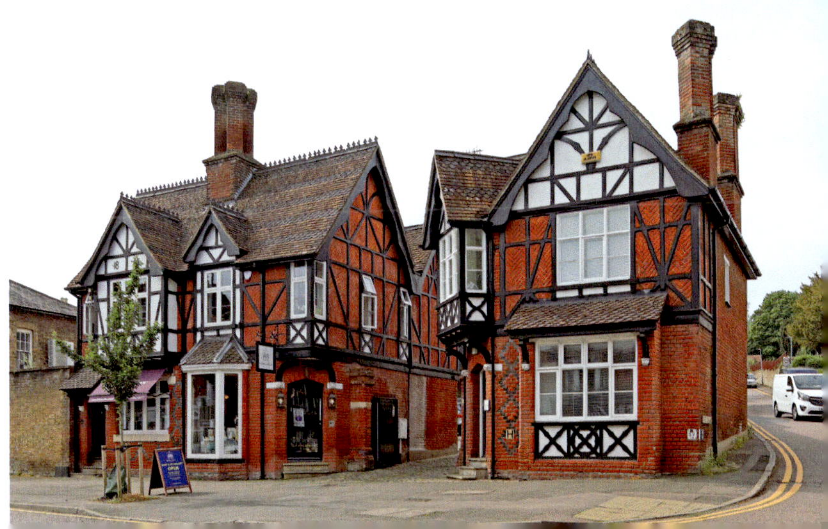

Nos 85–87 High Street, Victorian additions.

# The 50 Buildings



## 1. Berkhamsted Castle and Cottage

William the Conqueror accepted the submission of the English at Berkhamsted Castle after the Battle of Hastings. His half-brother, Robert of Mortain, constructed a timber castle there in around 1070. It was in the classic Norman motte-and-bailey form, with a defensive conical mound and oval bailey below.

The castle was to remain in royal hands, and in 1155 Thomas Becket was granted the honour of Berkhamsted by King Henry II. As chancellor, Becket was the king's right-hand man and enjoyed great favour. He rebuilt the castle to befit his new status and house his large staff. Becket's buildings probably included the huge stone curtain wall. Later in 1164, during his quarrel with the king, Becket was accused of embezzlement. He was disgraced and deprived of the honour of Berkhamsted.

Berkhamsted Castle was designed as a fortress, with impressive earthwork defences, a high motte and stone curtain wall. The water-filled ditches prevented tunnelling under the wall, and the motte could protect the bailey as well as defend attacks from the north. In 1216, the castle's defences were severely tested. Prince Louis of France had invaded England at the invitation of the English barons, who were opposed to King John. When John died in October 1216, his nine-year-old son was crowned King Henry III. Louis had to act quickly. Louis besieged the castle for two weeks, hammering it with huge stones flung from siege weapons. The earthwork buttresses by the outer ditch were probably platforms to support them, although it is still unclear which side built them. The castle surrendered finally on the orders of the king.

Berkhamsted Castle was then granted to Richard, Earl of Cornwall, in 1225 by his brother, King Henry III. Richard was believed to be the richest man in England and was also a skilful diplomat. He was often needed at the royal court in London. Richard made Berkhamsted the administrative centre of the earldom of Cornwall. Bailiffs from his numerous estates brought their accounts there. He repaired and refurbished the castle and enlarged the western tower to create a luxurious palace complex. Parts of the palace, believed to be the chapel and possibly the undercroft of the Great Painted Chamber, remain. Richard's son Edmund was born at the castle and two of his wives died there. He himself died at Berkhamsted in 1272.

A century later Edward, the Black Prince (1330–71), son and heir of Edward III, was given the castle as Duke of Cornwall. Berkhamsted was a favourite residence of the Black Prince, and he repaired the castle buildings and ordered a new timber palisade around the park to keep the deer from escaping. He married Joan, 'the Fair Maid of Kent', in 1361 and the couple spent their first Christmas at the castle.

The castle later passed to five queens in succession, ending with Elizabeth I. It was probably not occupied after 1495, however. When Elizabeth I granted a lease of the manor to Sir Edward Carey in 1580, he built a new house to the west – Berkhamsted Place – which is now almost totally demolished, while the castle itself gradually fell into ruin.

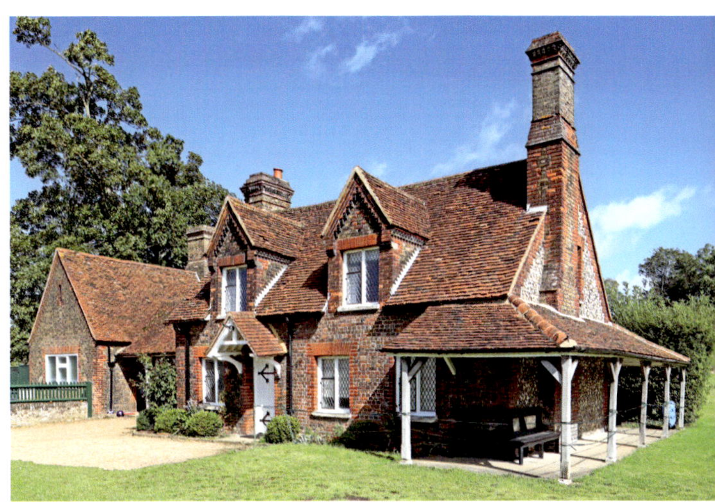

*Right*: The keeper's cottage within the ruins of Berkhamsted Castle, presumed to be the location of the Countess of Bridgewater's soup kitchen in the 1840s.

*Below*: The remains of Berkhamsted Castle and mound.

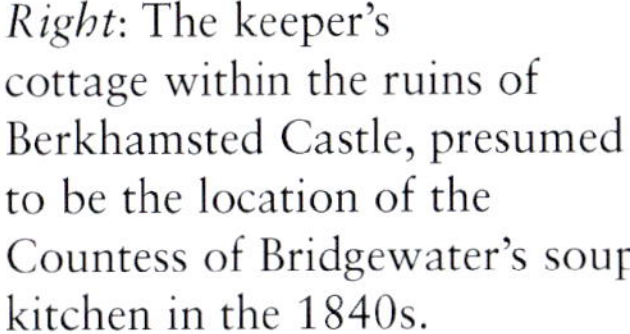

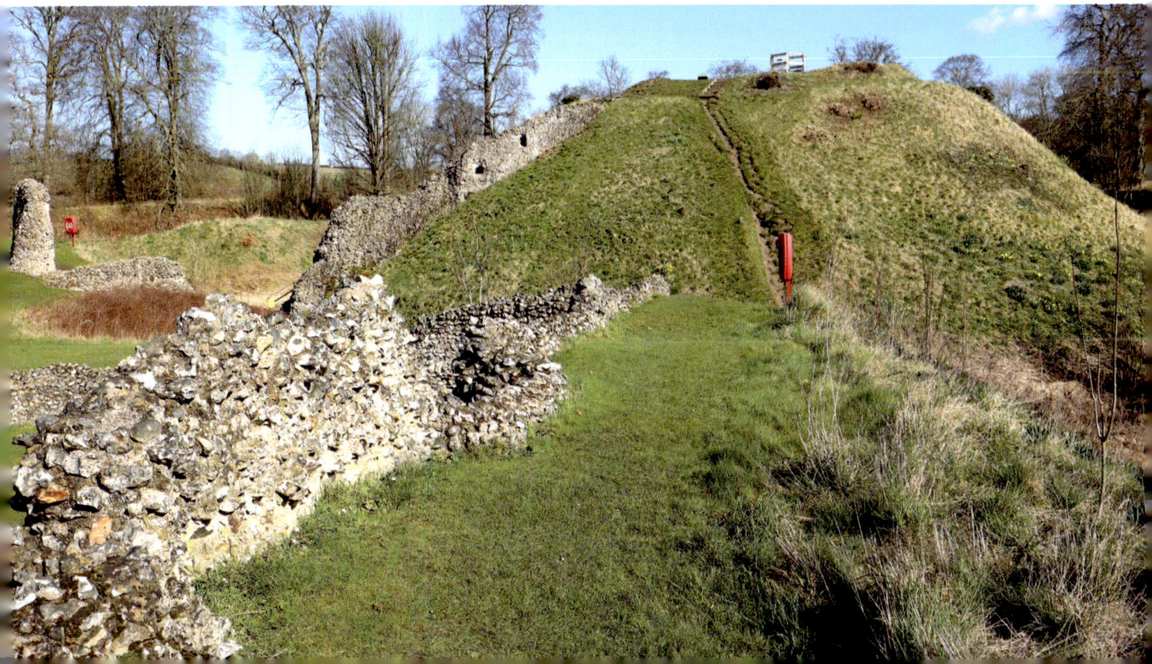

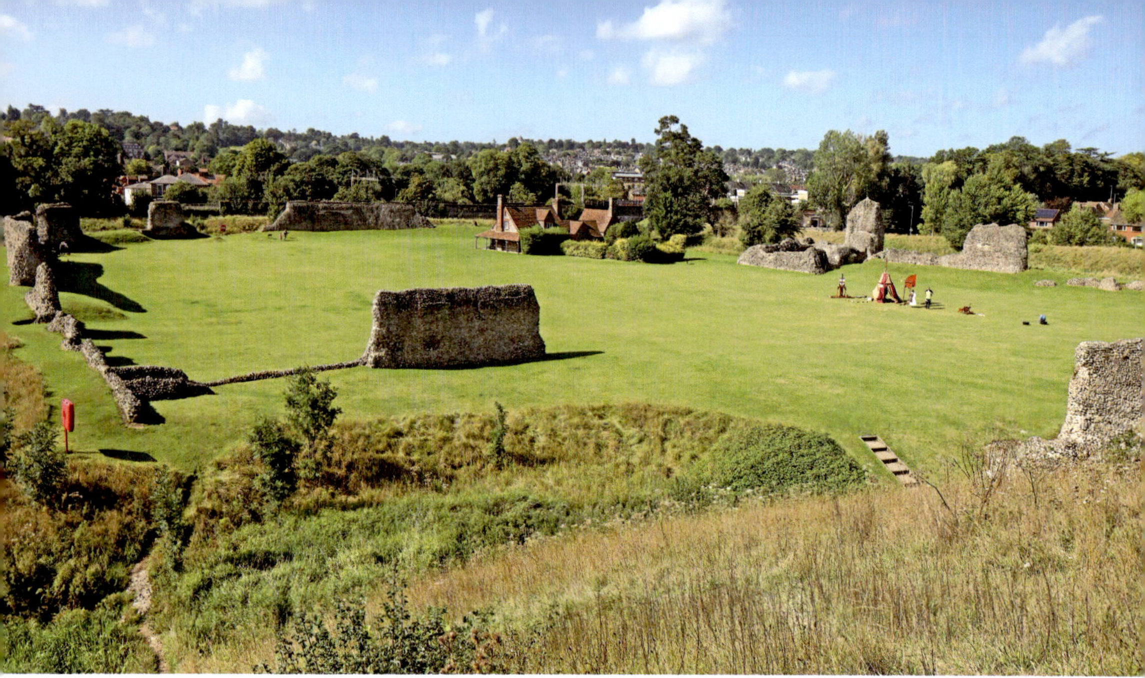

View from the castle mound.

## 2. St Mary's Church and Almshouses, Northchurch

Although considered by many to be a suburb of Berkhamsted, the village of Northchurch is in fact far older and very much part of the wider town. Roman occupation in this area dates from around AD 60 and was primarily devoted to agriculture, including the raising of cattle, sheep, pigs and goats.

Once the Romans had left the area the Saxons formed a settlement between the road and the river calling it 'Birch Hamsted'. The original church in this location dates from this time and makes St Mary's one of the oldest churches in Hertfordshire. Part of the original Saxon building still remains in the south and west walls. In early Norman times the parish was known as Berkhampstead St Mary and the entry in the Domesday Book relating to Berkhampstead refers to a priest with fourteen villeins (tenant farmers).

By the thirteenth century, buildings had extended south along the former Akeman Street towards the Norman castle and effectively became a separate settlement, taking with it the old name of Berkhampstead. The church of St Peter, in present-day Berkhamsted, dates from this time. With the creation of its own parish, Berkhampstead St Mary subsequently became known as 'Northcherche' or the North Church – the church to the north of St Peter's. The name of the village has since evolved into the current Northchurch.

St Mary's was subsequently extended eastwards between the eleventh and fourteenth centuries to form a cruciform building with flint walls. A stone-faced tower was added over the crossing during the fifteenth century. A new north aisle, vestries and south porch were added in the 1880s.

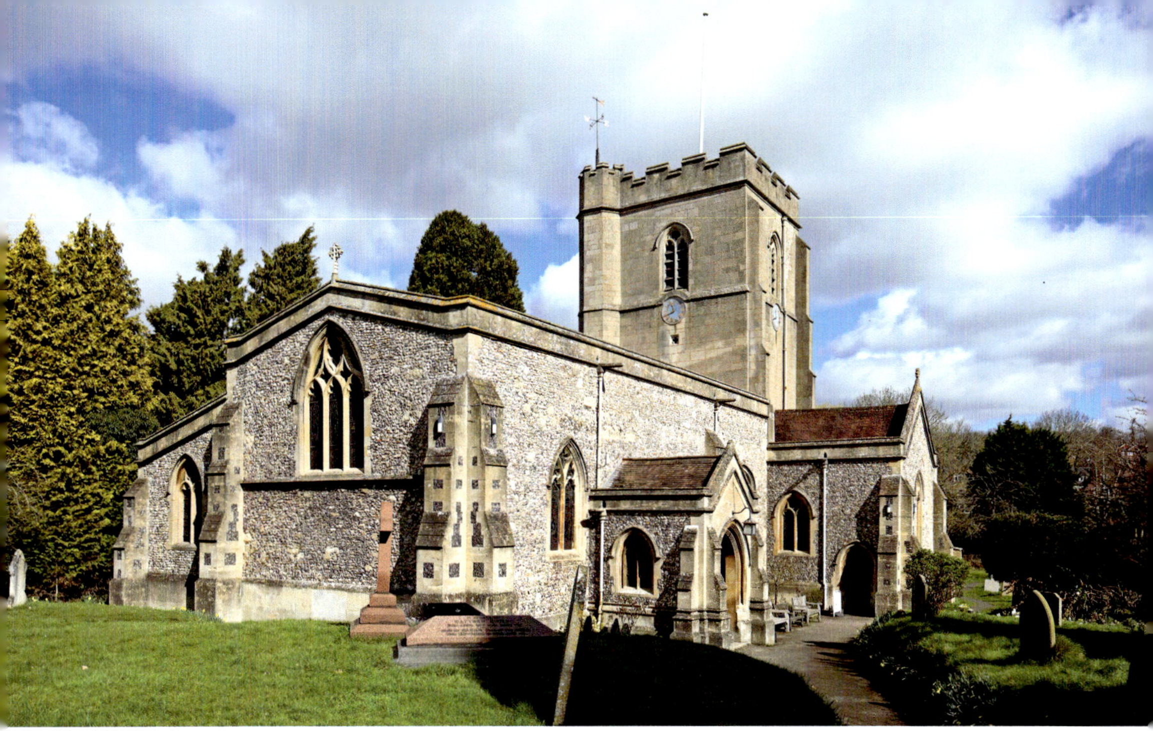

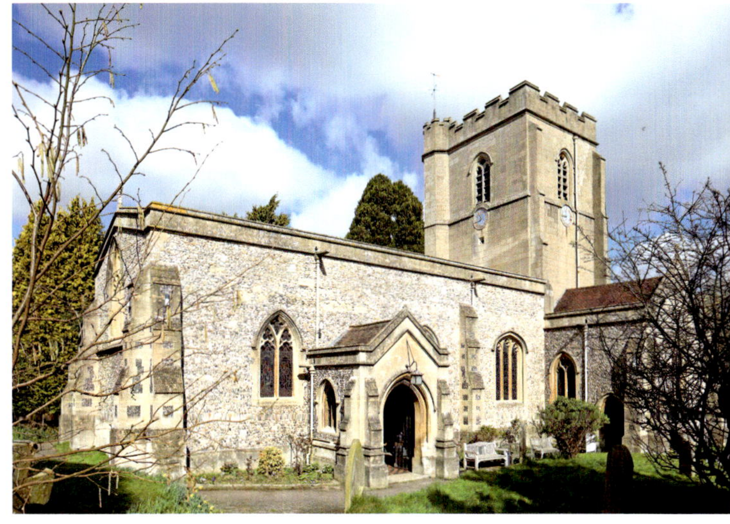

*Above*: St Mary's Church, one of the oldest in Hertfordshire.

*Right*: St Mary's Church and its flint walls.

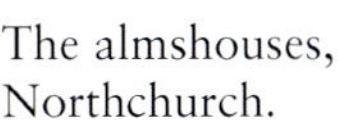

The almshouses, Northchurch.

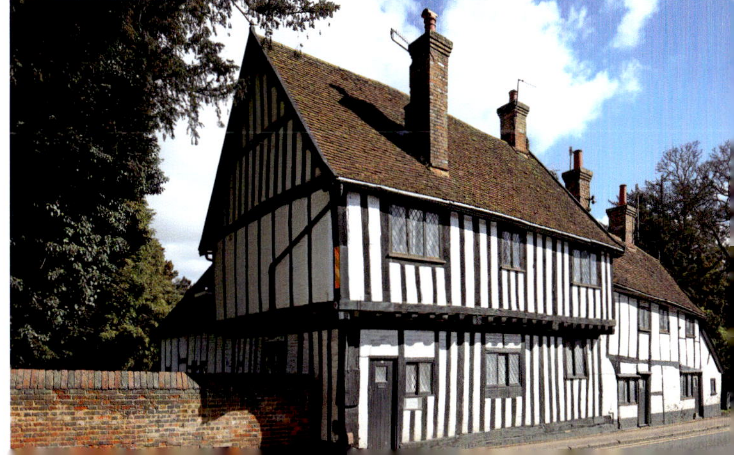

The internal decor of St Mary's reflects Victorian 'sensitivities', with renewed windows containing nineteenth and early twentieth-century stained glass. However, a major reordering project was undertaken in 1980, when the organ and choir stalls were moved from the north transept (now the Lady Chapel) to the west end of the church, and a nave altar constructed beneath the crossing. The Lady Chapel was refurbished in 1997 and a stained-glass window introduced into the south transept in 2000 to mark the new millennium.

Apart from St Mary's, probably the most well-known buildings in Northchurch are the almshouses or church houses. These two-storey half-timbered houses date from the fifteenth and sixteenth centuries and have recently been refurbished.


## 3. St Peter's Church

A church has existed on this site for nearly 800 years, and parish records stretch back to 1222. The church has stood through many significant periods of English history, including the Black Death, the Reformation, the Civil War, the Act of Union and two world wars. Within its grounds, the fortunes of the town can be traced in its many interesting and historically significant memorials and features. A number of monuments and memorial inscriptions survive from the medieval period. There are also memorials which commemorate departed parishioners who have been buried elsewhere, including in St Peter's Cemetery on Rectory Lane. Several burials in Rectory Lane Cemetery are important figures in the life of St Peter's Church.

During the incumbency of Revd James Hutchinson, a major restoration programme was commissioned from the noted Gothic Revival architect William Butterfield. Among many changes, he restored the crumbling exterior of the church with flint, raised the south transept roof and removed many ancient memorials. The noted eighteenth-century poet and hymn writer William Cowper

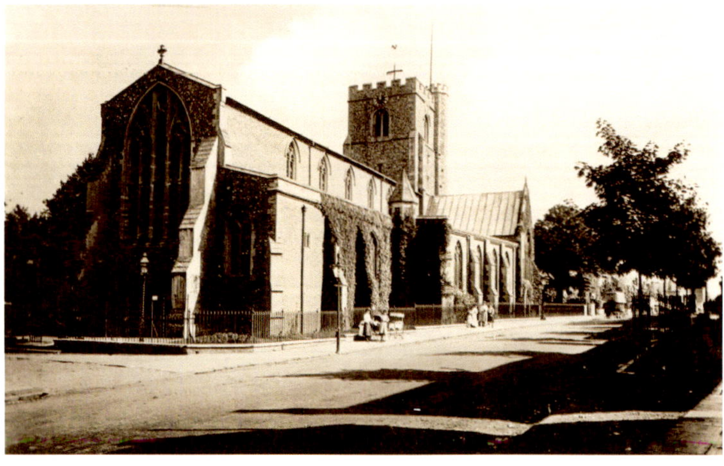

An Edwardian scene with St Peter's Church.

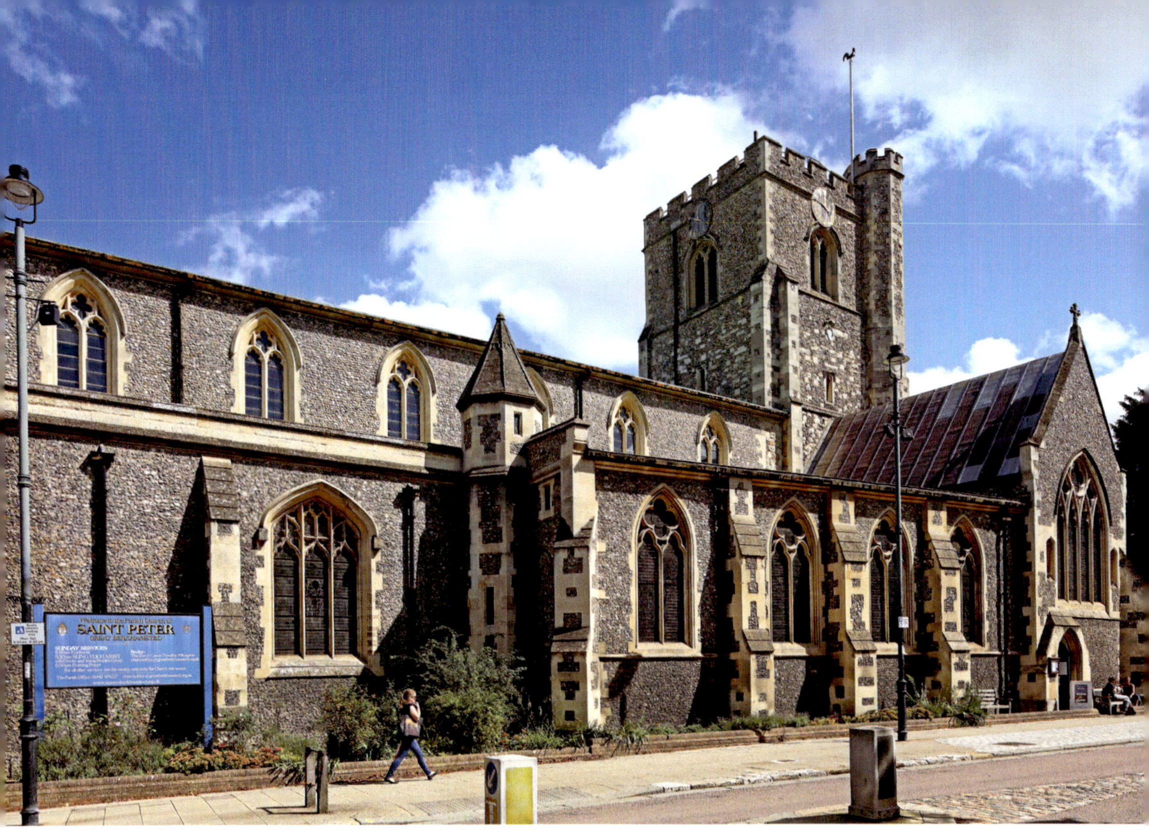

St Peter's Church. There has been a church here for many centuries.

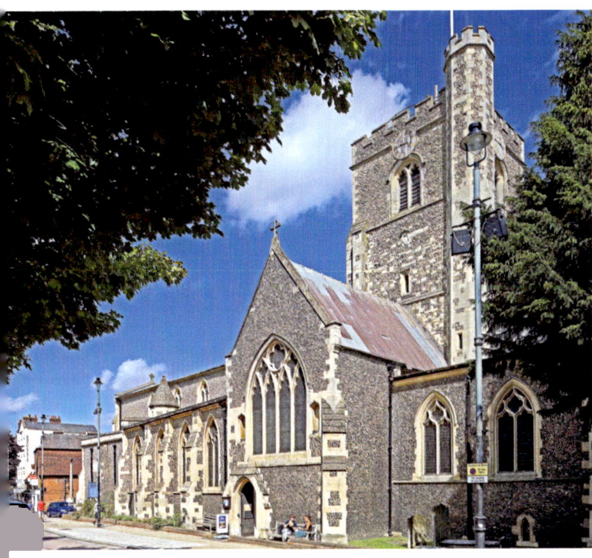

*Above*: St Peter's Church, one of the most important buildings in the town.

*Right*: Flint dominates the exterior of the church today.

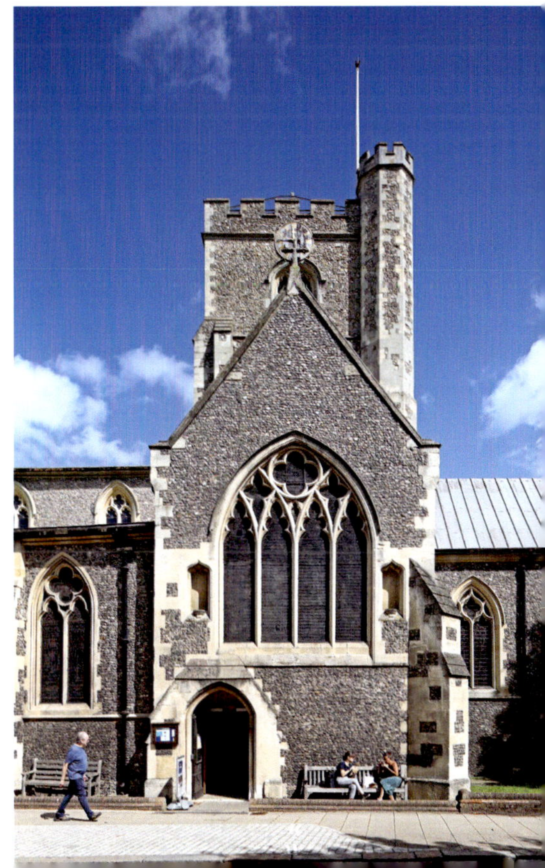

is also commemorated in two stained-glass windows in St Peter's Church. Cowper was the son of the rector of St Peter's, Revd John Cowper, and grew up in the rectory after which Rectory Lane is named.

## 4. No. 173 High Street

No. 173 High Street is considered to be the oldest surviving jettied timber-framed building in the country, dated between 1277 and 1297. At the time of the building's construction, the town of Berkhamsted was a relatively large, flourishing wool trading market town that benefited from having an important royal castle.

The building was given a Victorian façade and was used as a pharmacy in the nineteenth century. Its historical significance was not recognised until 2001 when it was Grade II* listed after the medieval timber framing was exposed during renovation work. It is currently used as an estate agents. Dr Simon Thurley, Chief Executive of English Heritage, was quoted: 'This is an amazing discovery. It gives an extraordinary insight into how Berkhamsted High Street would have looked in medieval times.'

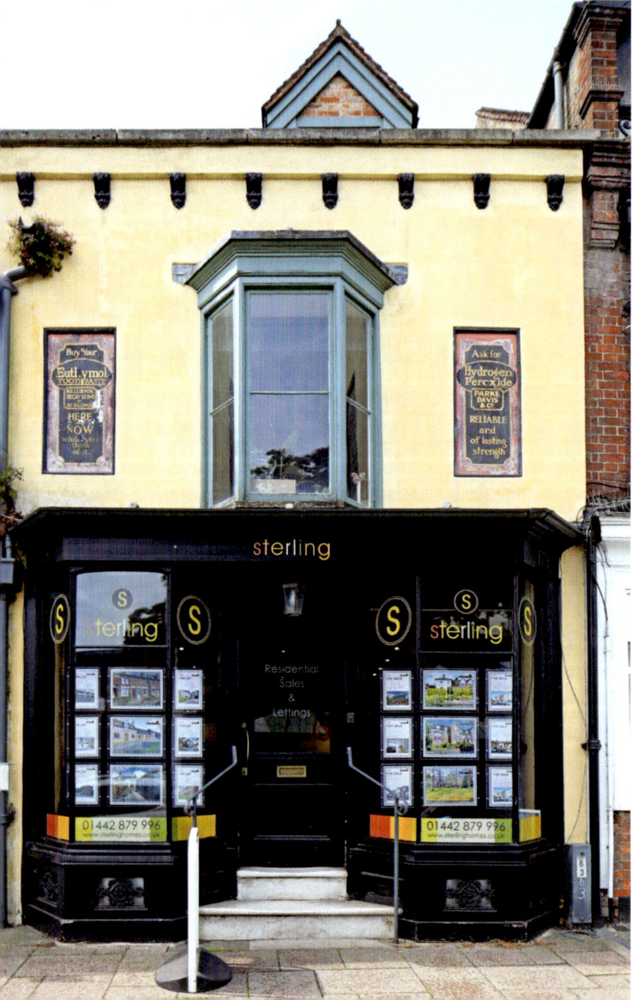


No. 173 High Street, the country's 'oldest' shop.

Initially, the investigations suggested that it had always been a shop, as there was evidence for the existence of a jeweller or goldsmith's shop with a workshop behind. This generated headlines to the effect that the country's 'oldest shop' had been discovered. The age of the building would make it a contender for the title, but there is doubt about how long it served as a shop. It is now believed to have originally been a jettied service wing to a larger aisled hall house, which has since disappeared.

## 5. Dean Incent's House

The oldest domestic building on Berkhamsted High Street is probably No. 173. However, Dean Incent's House has a rival claim. Evidence exists that an older medieval building stood to the rear of the house, at right angles to the High Street. Part of this older house was incorporated into the Tudor house, which was built facing the High Street. It is thought that the house may originally have been used as a public meeting hall before the construction of the Court House on the opposite side of the road.

In the late fifteenth century, this house belonged to Robert and Katherine Incent. They were a family of high standing in the town of Great Berkhamsted, Robert serving as secretary to Cicely, Duchess of York, the last royal resident at Berkhamsted Castle, wife of the Duke of York and mother of two kings of England, Edward IV and Richard III.

The house is named after the Incents' son, John Incent, a priest in the Church of England who served as chaplain to King Henry VIII during the time of Henry's divorce from Catherine of Aragon. In 1540, Incent was appointed by the king as dean of St Paul's Cathedral in recognition of his loyalty and service during the break with Rome. The Incent family are commemorated with memorials in the Church of St Peter, Great Berkhamsted, which stands on the High Street opposite Dean Incent's House.

In common with many high-ranking clergy at this time, John Incent founded a school in the town. Dean Incent's Free School in 'Berkhamstedde' was established in 1541 using land that he had appropriated from the monastic hospital of St John the Baptist during the Dissolution of the Monasteries. The school, which stands behind St Peter's Church, is still in existence today as the Berkhamsted School.

Around 1907–08, Dean Incent's House was occupied by local photographer James T. Newman, who had moved to Berkhamsted in 1888. Newman set up a studio in the house and shot many photographs of Berkhamsted, as well as photographs of the Inns of Court Regiment which was based in Berkhamsted during the First World War.

From 1930 to 1970, Dean Incent's House was used as a traditional tearoom and restaurant, after which it was used as accommodation for schoolmasters at Berkhamsted School. It has since been returned to use as a private dwelling. Nikolaus Pevsner described it as 'the best house in Berkhamsted'.

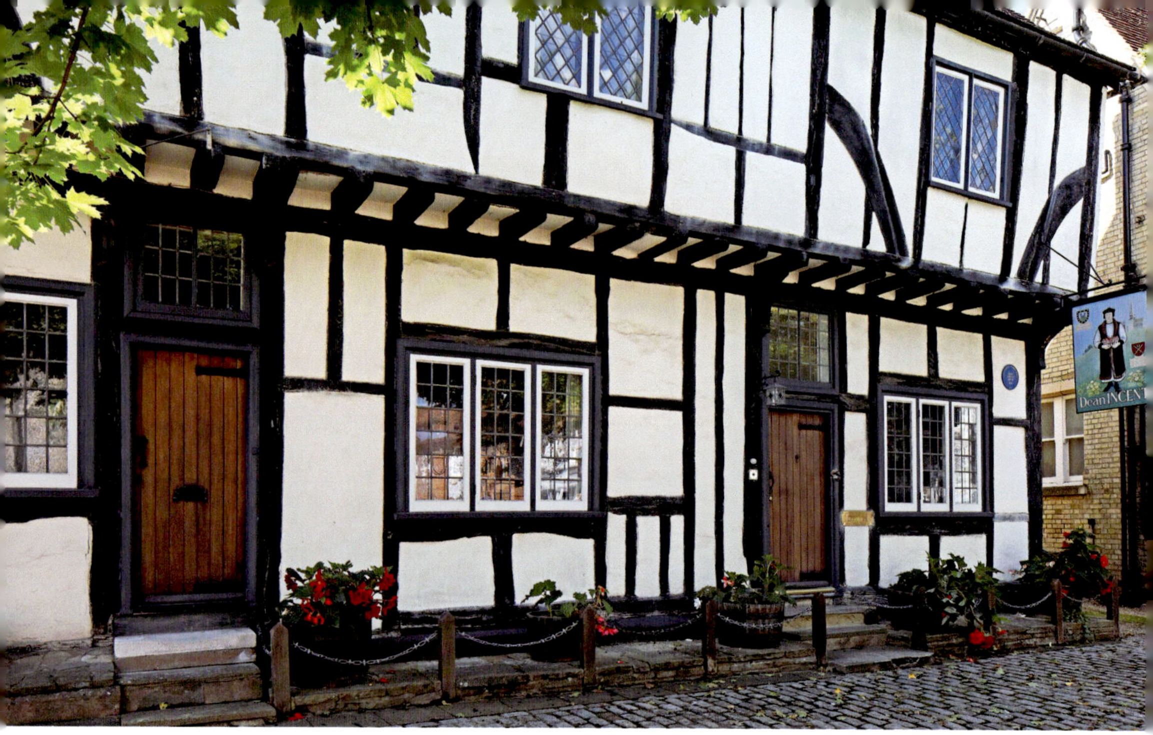

*Above and left*: Dean Incent's House, the 'best house in Berkhamsted'.

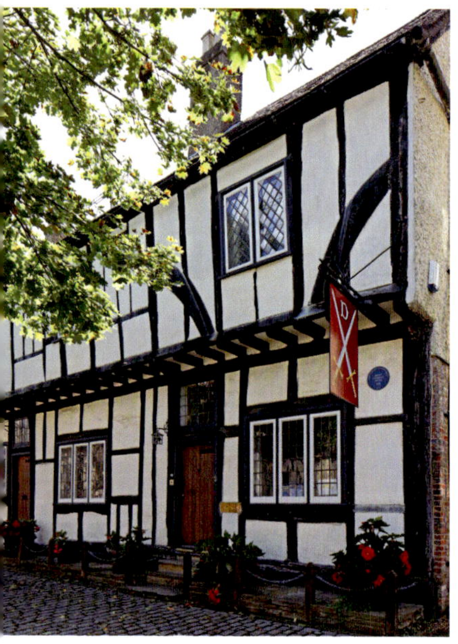

## 6. Berkhamsted School

Berkhamsted School is an independent school in the town. It was founded during the reign of Henry VIII, in 1541 by John Incent.

In 1541, he obtained a royal charter for 'one chauntry perpetual and schools for boys not exceeding 144 to be called Dean Incent's Free School in Berkhamstedde'.

It was common practice at this time for high-ranking clergy to make their mark by founding schools.

Incent 'builded with all speed a fair schoole lartge and great all of brick very sumptuously'. It was completed in 1544 'when ye said school was thus finished, ye Deane sent for ye cheafe men of ye towne into ye school where he kneeling gave thanks to Almighty God'.

Incent died eighteen months later. The school was incorporated by an Act of Parliament as 'The Free Schole of King Edwarde the Sixte in Berkhampstedde'. The school crest granted at the time – and still in use today – bears Incent's coat of arms: crossed swords on a blue shield.

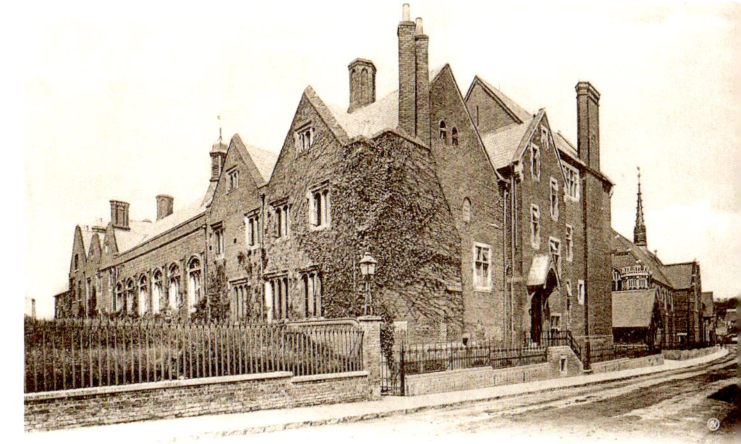

*Right*: An early postcard view of Berkhamsted School.

*Below*: The school resplendent in the Hertfordshire sunshine.

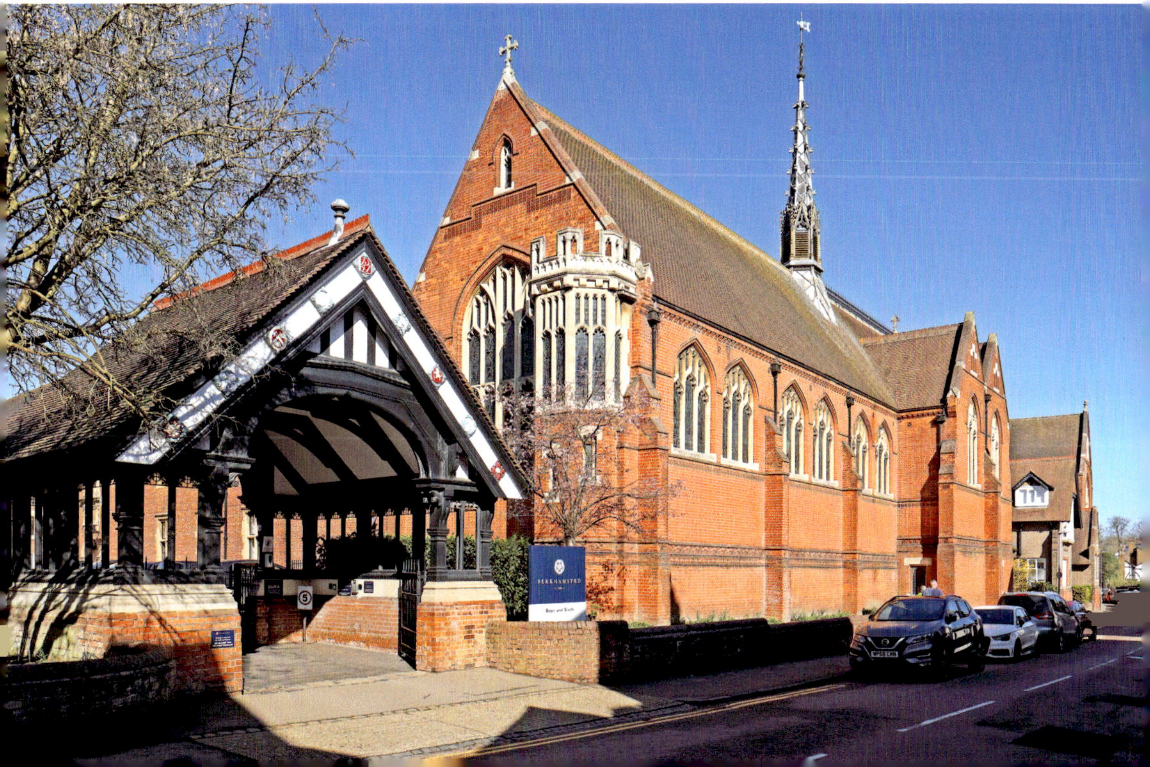

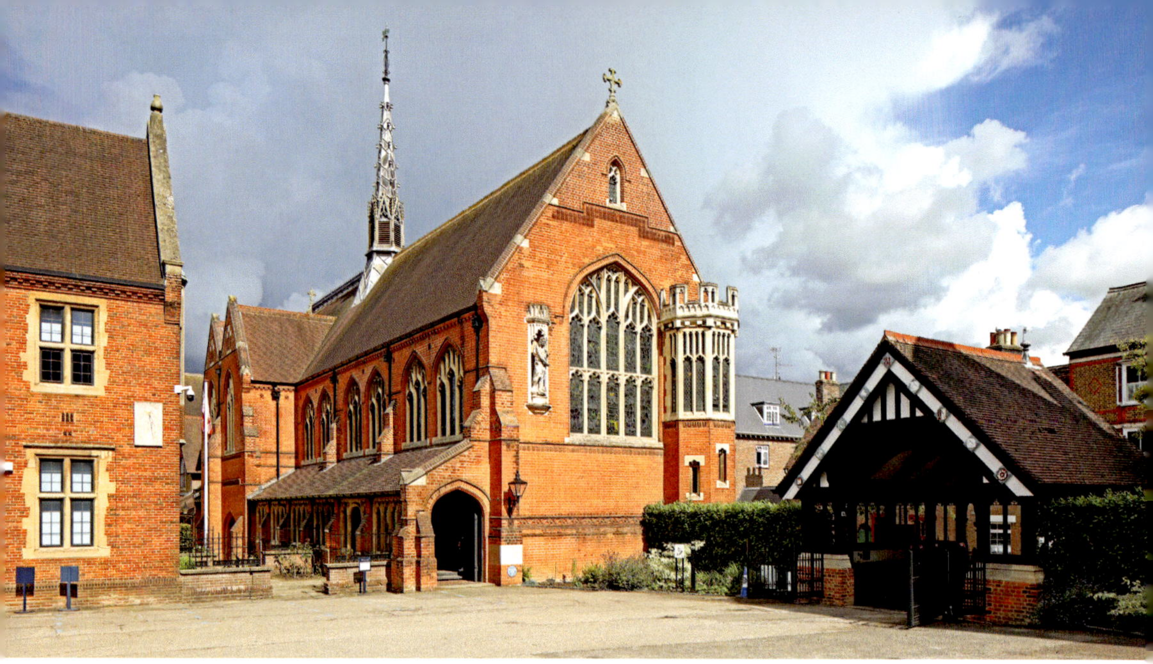

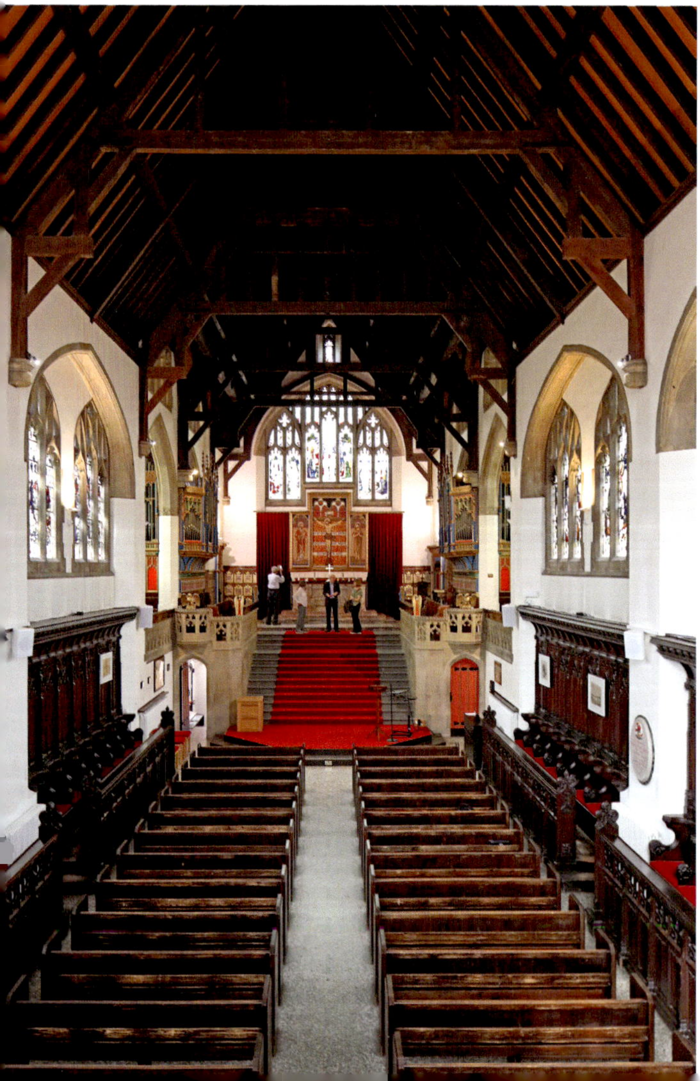

*Above*: The school chapel, built in 1894.

*Left*: The chapel interior.

Berkhamsted School had no chapel of its own. For over 300 years the St John's Chantry in neighbouring St Peter's Church was used exclusively by the masters and boys of the school for worship, until a new school chapel was built in 1894. It was designed in a Gothic Revival style by the local architect, Charles Henry Rew. The interior is quite unusual as the altar sits at top of a long flight of stairs. Rew based this layout on the design of the church of the Santa Maria dei Miracoli, Venice.

In 1997, Berkhamsted School amalgamated with the Berkhamsted School for Girls (established 1888) and Berkhamsted Preparatory School, and later with Heatherton House School in Amersham, and Haresfoot School in Berkhamsted.

Notable past headmasters have included Edward Bartrum (1864–89), whose wife, Caroline, is buried in Rectory Lane Cemetery, and Charles Henry Greene (1911–27), father of author Graham Greene.

*Right*: The school buildings.

*Below*: The central green area to Berkhamsted School.

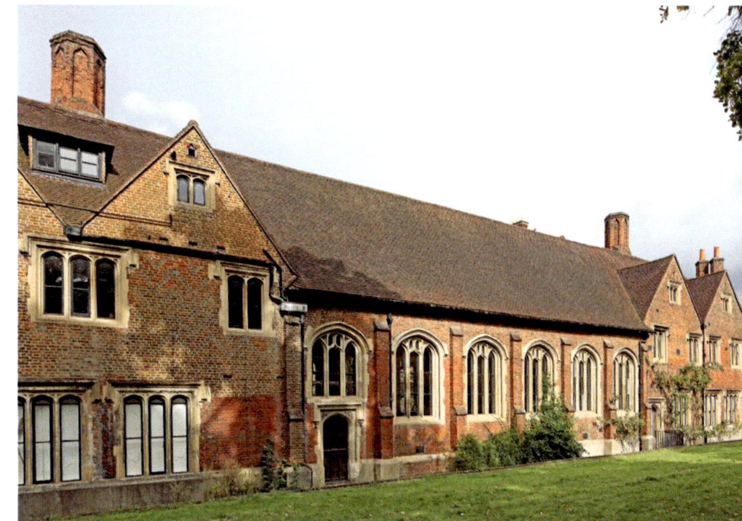

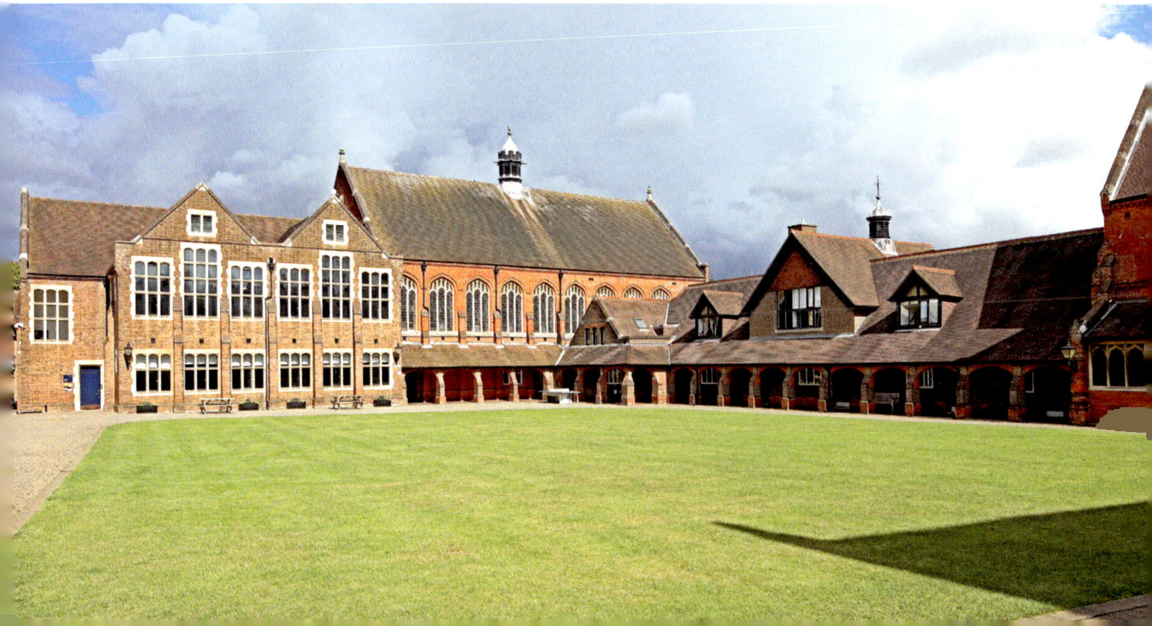

## 7. The Boote

The Boote bears the date '1605' and is a typical oak-framed building of its time. It was one of at least six pubs which existed in Castle Street at one time. Historically, Castle Street was the second most important thoroughfare in the town. Before the railway came it linked the High Street directly to the castle. The Boote was a public house until 1920 when it became a private home, after serving some time as an antiques business.

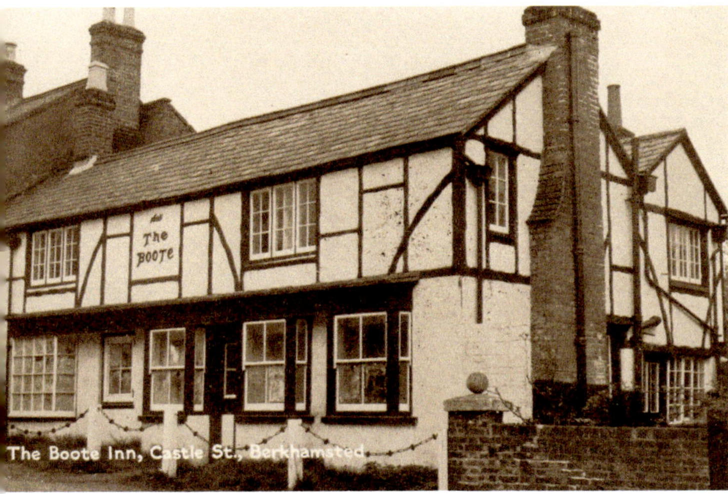


*Left*: An early historical view of the Boote Inn, from when it was still a public house.

*Below*: It is a private residence today, rather than a public house.

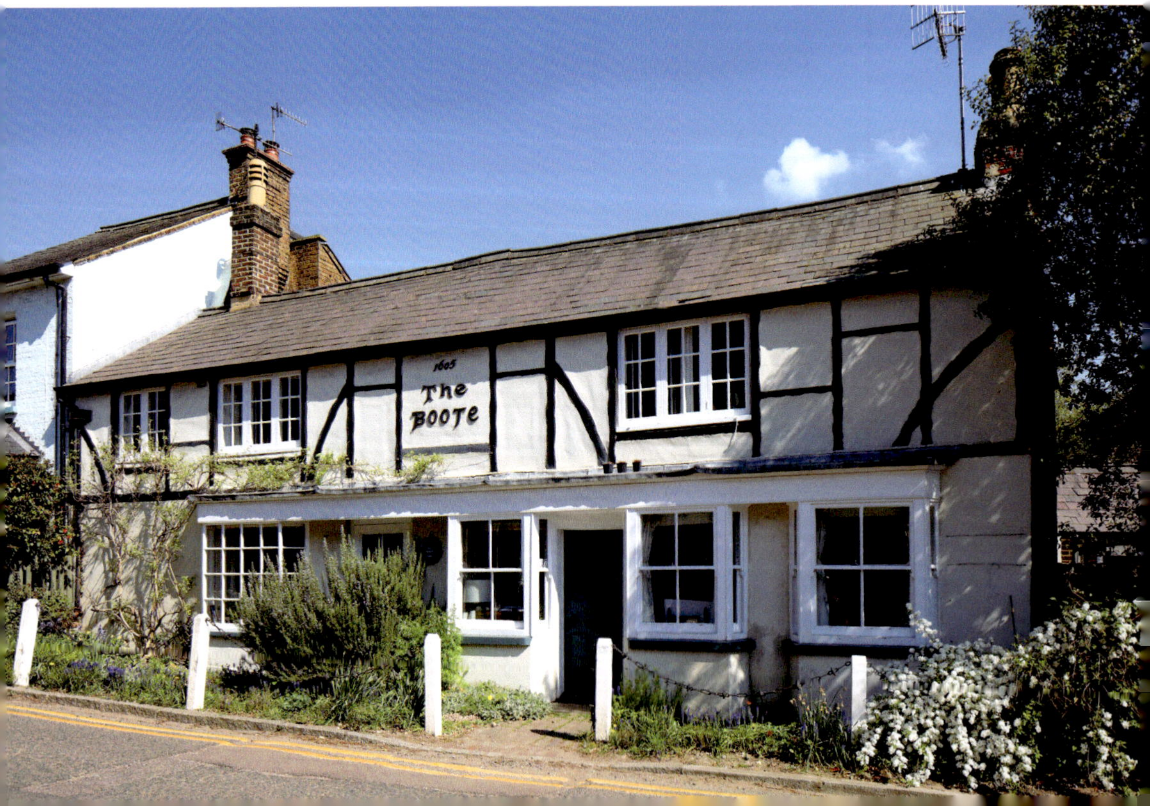

## S. Court House

The Court House is Tudor in origin but may well have been built on the site of a medieval building. It has also been known locally as the 'Church House' as well as the 'Town Hall'. In essence, it was the town's first centre of governance. The Common Council consisted at that time of a bailiff or mayor and twelve chief burgesses, who were elected annually. The council also had the services of a full-time recorder. This body was known as the Corporation. This town's charter, granted by James I, gave the town the right to hold a Court of Records at the Court House, where the Corporation also kept the standard weights and measures used to help settle trading disputes.

The Courts of the Manor and Honour of Berkhamsted were held traditionally on Whit Tuesday and on the Tuesday after Michaelmas. They met to hear 'all pleas, actions, suites or offences against the laws and liberty of the manor'. The Corporation were granted many powers, including permission to make bye-laws for the borough, as well as to impose fines, penalties and imprisonment, to have an extra market day every week and two additional fair days annually, to maintain a prison, and to collect market tolls. They were to hold a court of record once a month and a court of *pied poudre* to deal with petty offences on fair days.

Over many years the Court House has had a wide variety of uses. In 1838, it became the home of the National School, when additional rooms were built on the back of the house. Soon afterwards the cottage next door was built for the schoolmaster. However, this use was not to last. With the eventual introduction of the regulations of the 1870 Education Act and the Bourne Charity School children also joining the National School children, the premises in the Court House were no longer large enough. The Victoria Church of England Boys' School was built to commemorate Victoria's diamond jubilee. This was followed by the building of Victoria Girls' School, nearby, in the early 1900s.

In 1863, Earl Brownlow of Ashridge bought the Manor and Honour of Berkhamsted, with the exception of the castle, from the Duchy of Cornwall. This included the ownership of the Court House, which was immediately leased back to various trustees at a nominal rent. In 1898 the Berkhamsted Urban District Council was formed. Court sessions were held in the Sessions Hall at the Town Hall until the new Civic Centre was built in 1935.

During the First World War, a large contingent of Inns of Court Officers' Training Corps was billeted in the town from 1914 to 1919 when the Court House was then used as an orderly room for them. After the war, and during the Spanish flu epidemic the Court House was used as an extension hospital when local hospitals could not accommodate all the patients.

During the Second World War, like many rural towns, Berkhamsted had to accommodate many evacuees from London schools and half-time schooling became a requirement of the Court House, along with every other hall in the town which was used to accommodate the sudden surge in population. During the

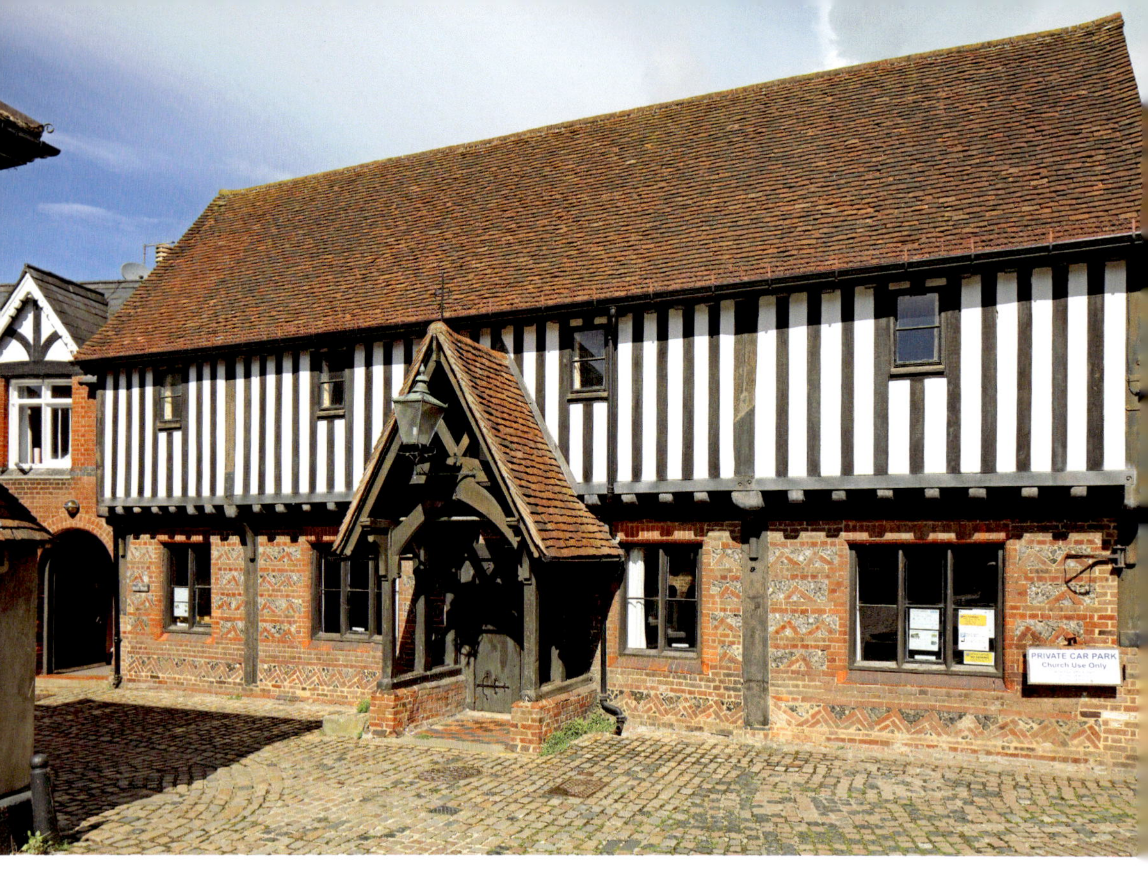

The old Court House, tucked away, is a very fine building of local importance.

late 1960s and early 1970s when the Victoria Schools were undergoing building works the children walked down the High Street in 'crocodiles' (two by two) to have lunch in St Peter's Hall behind the Court House. With the completion of the school building and the opening of their new hall, the old one became the dining hall and the Court House was refurbished and offices built behind, as we know it today. The Court House is now effectively the Church Hall for St Peter's Church.

## 9. The Swan Inn

The Swan is a former coaching inn on the corner of Berkhamsted High Street and Chesham Road (formerly Grubbs Lane). Dating from the sixteenth or seventeenth century, it is possible that this building was originally a row of three inns that were later joined together.

At the time the Swan was built, Berkhamsted High Street lay on an important stagecoach route. Coaches travelling from London to Tring, Banbury and Birmingham passed through Berkhamsted, and wealthy passengers brought trade to the town, stopping here for food and lodgings. The Universal British Directory of 1791 states that four coaches a week went between the Swan Inn and the Bell and Crown in Holborn.

Originally, the Swan had a small brewery and malting at the back of the premises. It was bought by George and Charles Foster in 1817 and was later owned by James Foster 1839–50. In 1853, it was acquired by a noted Berkhamsted entrepreneur John Edward Lane Sr (1808–89). Lane was well known nationally as a horticulturalist, and the family firm John Lane Nurseries supplied plants to parks and gardens all over the country. He expanded his business interests into beer brewing and acquired several pubs. The Swan is one of a chain of former John Lane pubs in Berkhamsted; the others are the Brownlow Arms, the Crystal Palace and the George.

Lane ran the Swan until 1871, when he sold it, along with the Brownlow Arms and the George, to Henry James Foster. Lane died in 1889 and was buried in Rectory Lane Cemetery.

In the late twentieth century the Swan ceased trading as a pub. In 1996, the dilapidated building was renovated and reopened as a youth centre.

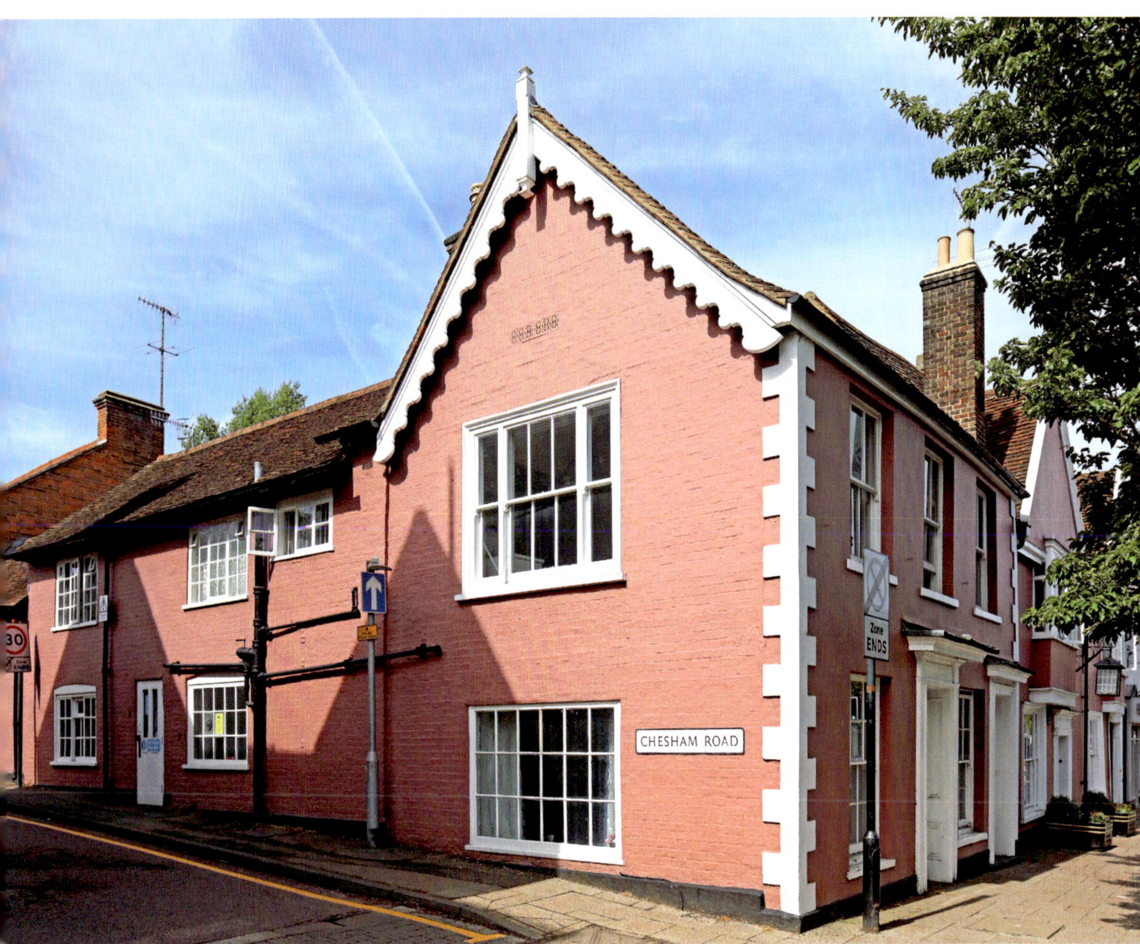


The former Swan Inn.

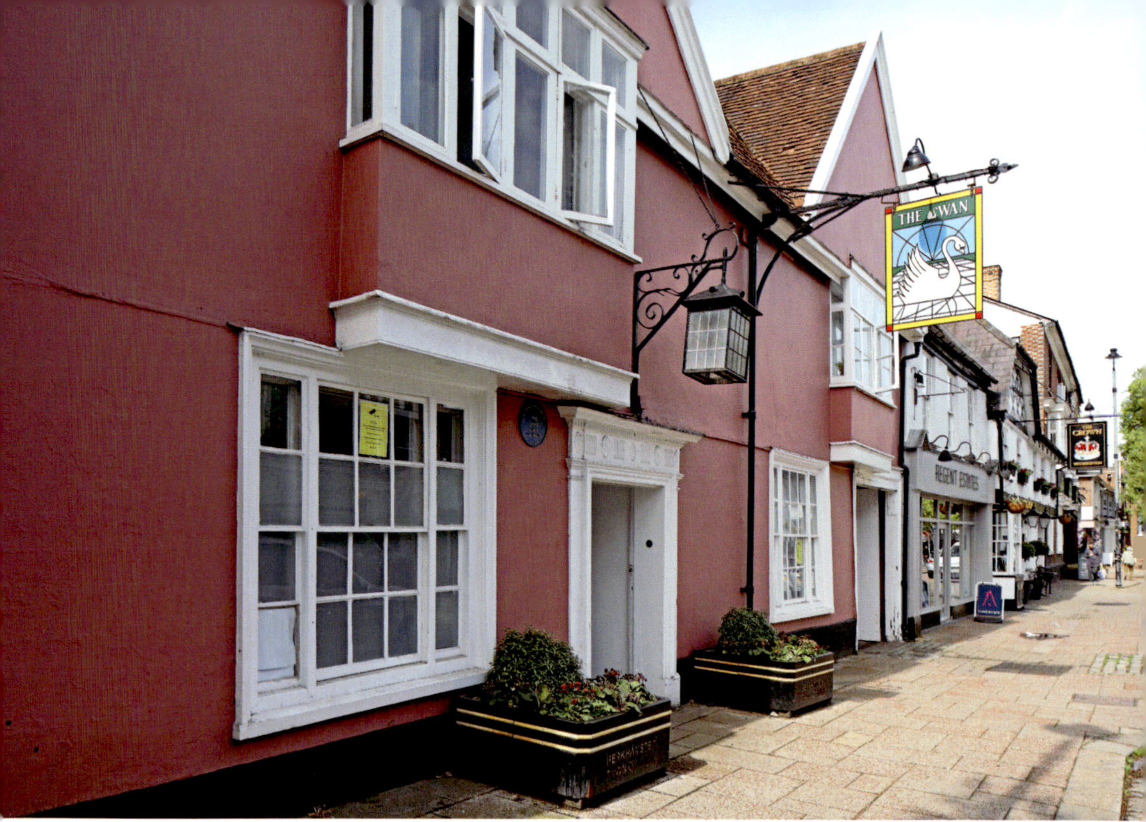

The former Swan Inn with a sign still in place hinting at its history as a popular public house.

## 10. The Kings Arms

Studying the history of buildings often reveals fascinating stories of not just the building, but those who lived within them at some time during their history. This can be said for the Kings Arms in Berkhamsted. The inn is thought to have been built in the late seventeenth or early eighteenth century, during the reign of Queen Anne. At this time, Britain's transport network was expanding and stagecoaches plied their trade along Akeman Street between London and the north. This created demand for overnight accommodation, and a network of coaching inns sprang up all over the country.

The Kings Arms here in Berkhamsted became a popular stop for coaches on their way between Tring and the Bell and Crown in Holborn, and coaches heading for Banbury and Birmingham. Here, the travelling gentry could change or rest horses, since there was stabling for up to forty horses as well as coach houses and facilities for harness storage. The Universal British Directory of 1791 designated the Kings Arms as the best inn in the town.

From 1792 to 1840, the landlord of the Kings Arms was innkeeper John Page. He and his wife Mary ran the inn for fifty-three years. The inn flourished under their management and the Kings Arms became a social hotspot frequented by the gentry. He provided a room 'most tastefully fitted up with artificial flowers and laurels' and provided musical entertainment.

However, one of the main attractions of the Kings Arms were John Page's three very attractive daughters, Mary, Sarah and Catherine, and especially the eldest, Mary, who was always known as Polly. In the 1800s Polly became the talk of the town when she became closely acquainted with King Louis XVIII of France, who was in living exile at Hartwell House near Aylesbury between 1807 and 1814. Louis often made a point of changing or resting his horses at the Kings Arms en route to London to clearly visit Polly Page. Rumours proliferated of a romance, and the affair was even reported in *The Times*, who described Polly as 'the sprightly, chatting entertainer of King Louis XVIII'. John Page doubtless encouraged this since these royal visits were certainly helpful in attracting a superior clientele.

It is reported that after Louis XVIII was restored to power he invited Polly to visit him at the Palace of Versailles, which led to some malicious gossip. Polly denied the rumours and stated that 'nothing improprietous had taken place'.

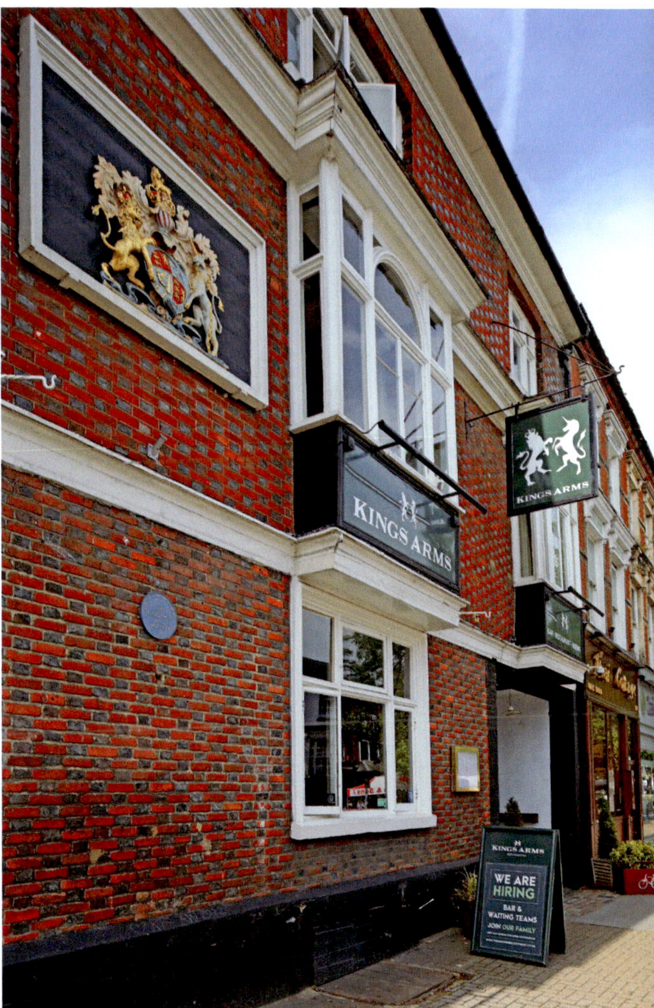

The Kings Arms, a former coaching inn with a French connection.

John Page died in 1840 and the running of the inn passed into Polly's hands. She was a capable and hardworking businesswoman, and the Kings Arms continued to attract a noble clientele. In 1841, Polly welcomed Queen Victoria and Prince Albert when they changed horses at Berkhamsted, on their way to visit the Duke of Bedford at Woburn. The townspeople made an elaborate decorated arch across the road to welcome the royals, and the party took refreshment at the Kings Arms. Polly managed the inn for a further twenty-five years before her death in 1865.

The advent of the railways in the 1830s created a threat to Britain's thriving stagecoaches, and also to coaching inns such as Polly Page's pub. Angry landowners held a protest meeting at the Kings Arms to object to the London & Birmingham Railway's plans to drive a new railway line across their country estates. Although they managed to influence the route, the controversial railway went ahead, and Berkhamsted railway station opened to passengers in 1837.

Despite the decline of coaching, the Kings Arms has remained in business for nearly 200 years.

## 11. Sayer's Almshouse

Almshouses were one of the earliest kinds of social housing, with their history stretching as far back as the tenth century. Their purpose was to enable elderly people who could no longer earn enough to pay rent to continue to live within their communities. The history of the John Sayer Almshouses in Berkhamsted is fascinating. They have been located in the centre of the town for over 300 years and are still in use today as originally intended.

But who was John Sayer? He was a loyal adherent to Charles II during his exile and became his chief cook after the Restoration and lived in Berkhamsted Place. Sayer was well connected and had many acquaintances, including the diarist Samuel Pepys who recorded the following passage in September 1661:

> I went with Captain Morrice into the King's Privy Kitchen to Mr Sayers, the master Cook, and there had a good slice of beef or two to our breakfast; and from thence he took us into the wine cellar where, by my troth, we were very merry, and I drank so much wine that I was not fit for business.

Sayer died in 1681 and in his will he bequeathed £1,000 in trust 'for the building of an almshouse and the purchasing of lands for the relief of the poor in Berkhamsted St Peter'. He did not live long enough to finalise the details. His black and white marble tomb is found in the Lady Chapel of St Peter's Church.

The beneficiaries who lived here were six poor widows, aged over fifty-five, and were constant frequenters of the Church of England, although this was later changed to just being Christians. However, they had to be single women and members of the Church of England. Other conditions applied too, including they must have lived in Berkhamsted for ten years and be at least fifty-five years of age. Each widow was awarded 8*s* a month and a cloth gown every three years. Only one widow could be absent at any one time, and for no longer than one month in any year. They had to attend church every Sunday, and at all times walk there in pairs. There were consequences as failure to do so meant a threepence fine; regular failure could lead to permanent exclusion. The youngest widow also had to look after the sick, and open and unlock the gates at specific times. Failure in this instance would lead to a 2*s* fine, with possible permanent exclusion after reprimands.

Despite the benevolence of John Sayer at the time, he was once regarded with contempt by many of the local townsfolk when he started interfering with the ancient rights of Berkhamsted. Revenues were diverted from the church, the 'Free School' and the poor. In desperation the rector, churchwardens and schoolmasters felt bound to petition Charles II, pointing out how Sayer 'doth much trouble your petitioners with suites in your Majesties name, under pretence of a grant from your Majestie'. The case was tried and Sayer won the day, but only at the expense of a further slump in his reputation locally. He was contemptuously referred to as the 'head cook and bottle-washer' as well as 'being Master of the Household, or Head Cook, to Charles II'. Despite this blemish on his character, his building remains as a testament to his generosity.

Sayer's Almshouse.

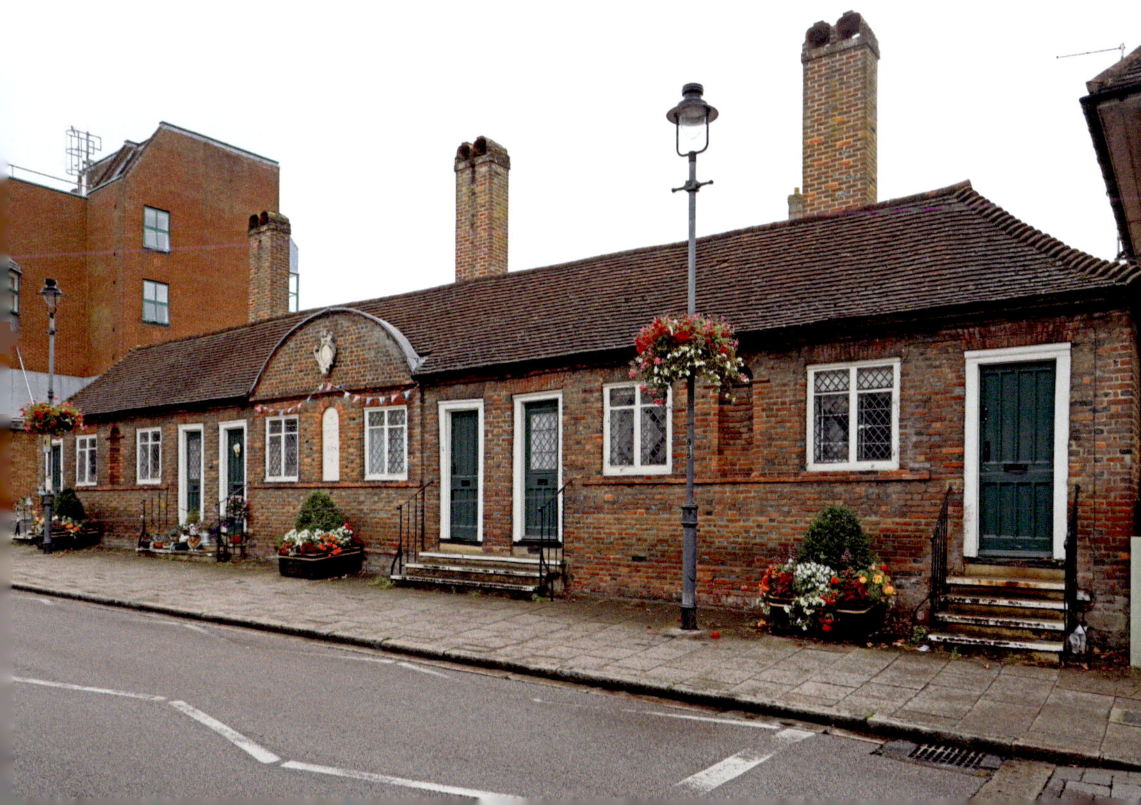

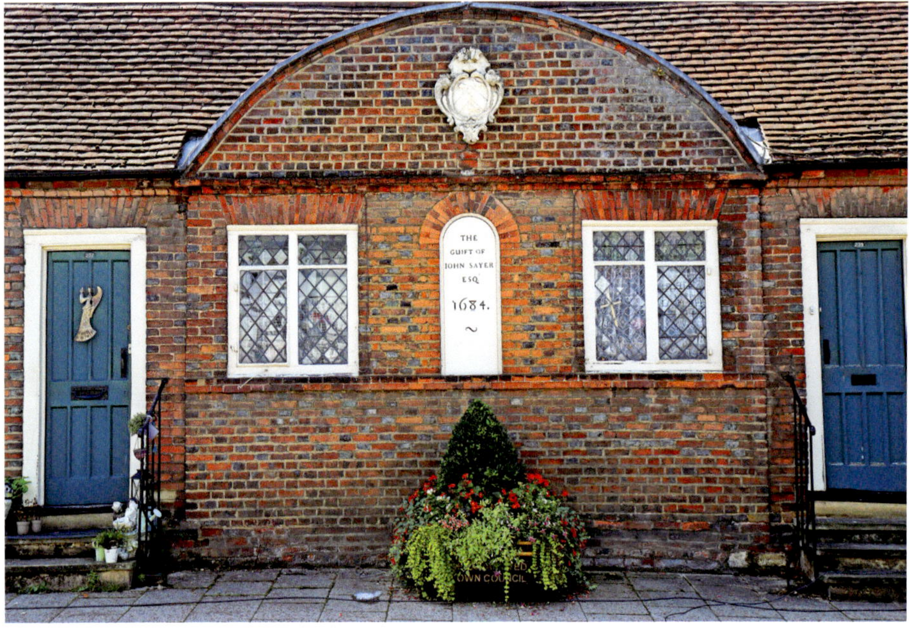

The gift of John Sayer Esq., 1684.

## 12. Former William Cowper's School

All along the High Street the original façades of the old houses can be seen above the modern shopfronts. In this location, a single shop (currently closed) has been made from three houses, the middle one of which dates from the early eighteenth century – William Cowper went to school here. One of the most popular poets of his time, Cowper changed the direction of eighteenth-century nature poetry by writing of everyday life and scenes of the English countryside. In many ways, he was one of the forerunners of Romantic poetry. Samuel Taylor Coleridge called him 'the best modern poet', whilst William Wordsworth particularly admired his poem 'Yardley-Oak'.

Cowper was born on 15 November 1731 at Berkhamsted, a child of Revd John Cowper and his first wife Ann (Donne). His grandfather was Spencer Cowper, the politician. In 1742, he entered Westminster School and then took up a legal career, which he hated. At the start of his literary career, he wrote essays for *The Connoisseur*. He was not allowed to marry his sweetheart, and he suffered depression and attempted suicide before he was suddenly converted. His first book of poems appeared in 1782. The best known is *The Task*. His hymn 'God Moves in a Mysterious Way' is still popular.

He died on 25 April 1800 and was buried at St Nicholas Church, East Dereham, Norfolk.

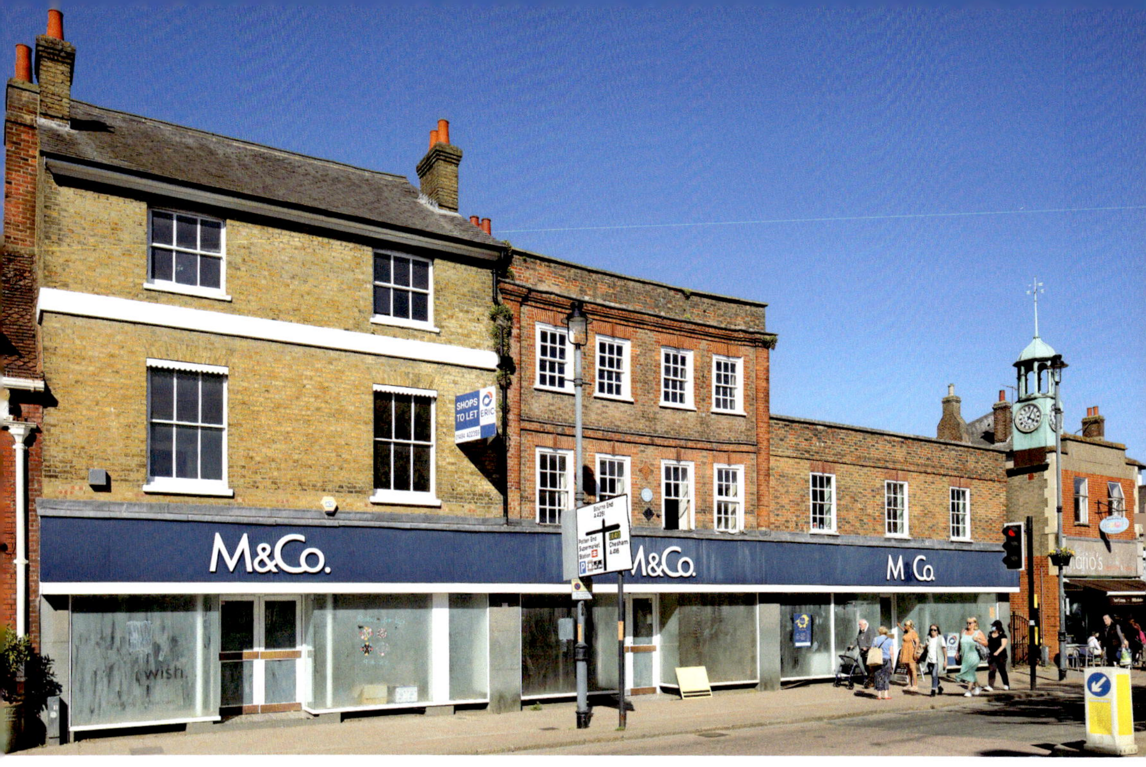

Now a run-down shop frontage but once an important educational institution where William Cowper attended.

## 13. The Former Bourne School

The Thomas Bourne Educational Foundation was established in 1729, on the death of Thomas Bourne of Camberwell. In his will and codicil, he left to the parish of Berkhamsted the sum of £8,000 to build and endow a charity school for twenty boys and ten girls. The bequest of such a large sum of money was remarkable in that Bourne was not a resident of Berkhamsted but only visited his sister, Sarah Rolfe, there occasionally. The executor, however, delayed settling the estate to such an extent that the then rector, Revd John Cowper, took out legal proceedings against them, and in 1735 the Attorney General ordered the payment of the legacy. The sum of £700 was then spent on building the school.

The school opened in 1737 and, as Bourne had directed, the boys were 'taught to read English, write and cast accounts' and the girls to read and then to do whatever work the churchwardens felt fit for them; they were not taught to write until 1761. Each pupil was given a new uniform annually and the parents of each child were given 1*s* or 1*s* 6*d* per week, depending on the state of the funds. Payments, however, were so in arrears by 1750 that the Court of Chancery appointed a receiver, and it is his account books that constitute the bulk of the collection (£2 1*s* 9*d*). The trustees met regularly to administer the foundation.

In 1853 a new classroom was added to the school mainly through the generosity of General John Finch. In 1875, however, the pupils of Bourne School were transferred to the National School and the money was awarded to scholars and exhibitioners passing the Bourne School examination. In 1888, the Bourne School became the first home of Berkhamsted School for Girls.

In 1949, however, with the agreement of the Charity Commissioners, no more scholars were appointed but the number of grants and exhibitions to boys and girls attending grammar schools, or other places of secondary or further education or training were increased.

The three coats of arms over the front door are those of Berkhamsted Town, Thomas Bourne and John Finch. The building was used by the Britannia Building Society for a number of years, but it is now a popular restaurant.

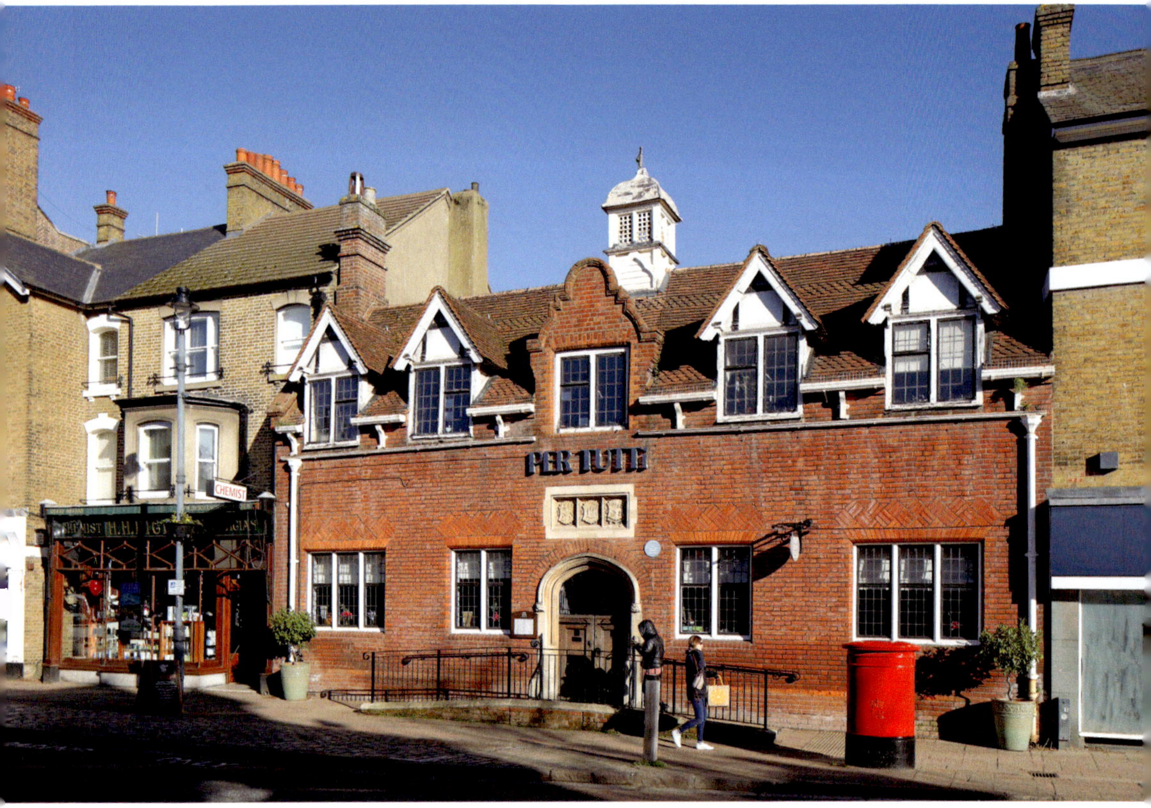

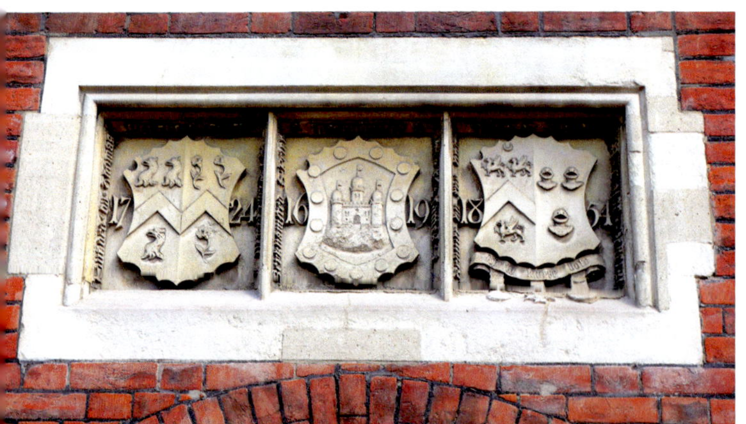

*Above*: The former Bourne School on the High Street.

*Left*: Three coats of arms above the front door to the old school.

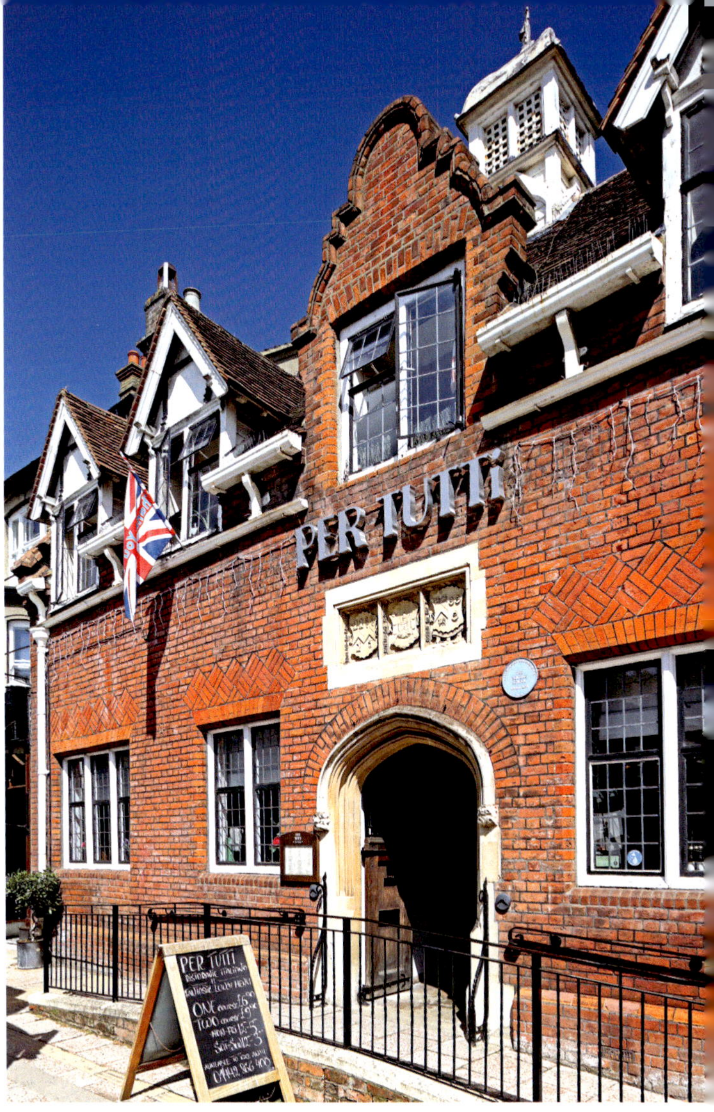

The old school, now a popular restaurant.

## 14. The George Inn

Berkhamsted High Street is well known for its many historical coaching inns and public houses. The George Inn is a late eighteenth-century coaching inn at the western end of the High Street, close to the corner of Park View Road. The bay window on the right side of the building was once a carriage entrance that led through to the back yard but has since been altered. Given the date of the pub, it seems likely that it was named after King George III, and his image appears on the pub sign today.

In the 1850s, the George Inn was bought by the local entrepreneur John Edward Lane Sr (1808–89). In the 1860s and 1870s it appears that the George Inn was being run by a Belgian, Pierre Wille (1829–90), who lived here with his wife Sarah Ann and their children. Wille was also a gardener, and was probably employed by Lane.

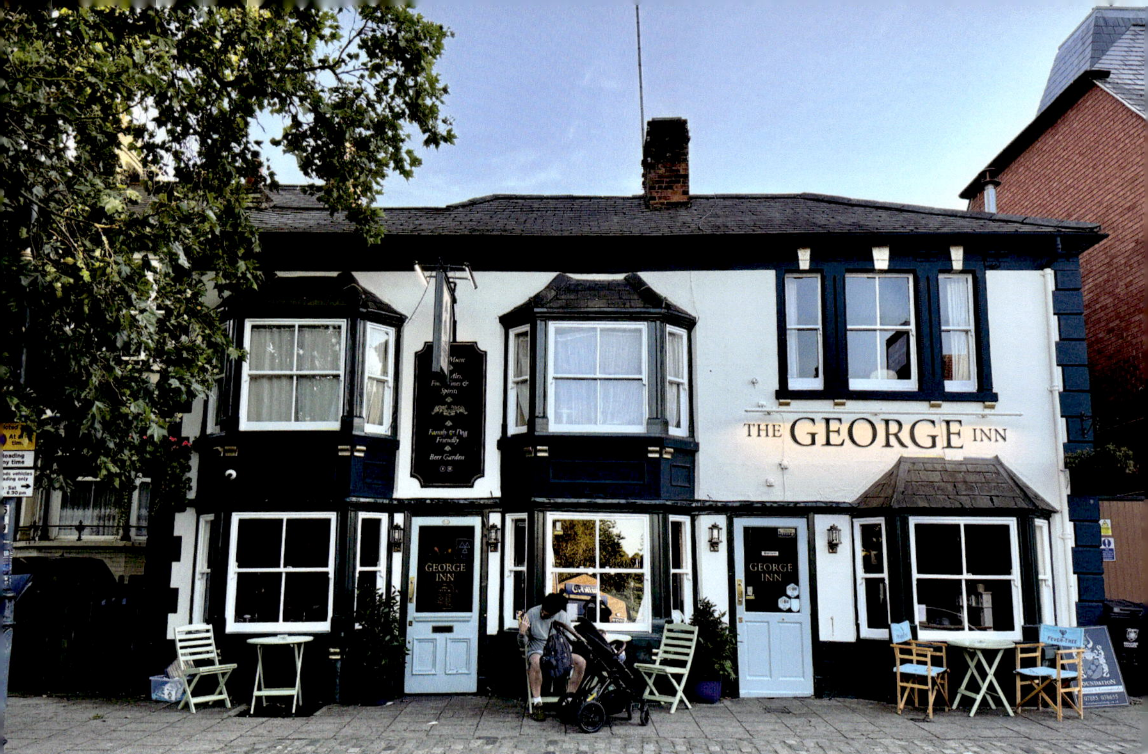

The George Inn.

## 15. Lock-keepers Cottage, Grand Union Canal

One of the driving forces of the early Industrial Revolution was the widespread construction of a network of canals throughout Britain, enabling for the first time the mass transportation of coal, materials and goods and spurring the advance of manufacturing and technological development.

A well-known figure in the history of Berkhamsted is Francis Egerton, 3rd Duke of Bridgewater (1736–1803), who lived at Ashridge. He is famously known as the 'Canal Duke' or the 'Father of Inland Navigation' because he made (and later lost) his fortune in building Britain's first canals in north-west England.

However, the canal we see today in Berkhamsted was not his work, but was constructed by his rivals, the Grand Junction Canal Company 1793–1805. The company drove a new canal between the Midlands and London, reaching Berkhamsted in 1798. The canal brought new employment and business opportunities to the town – townsfolk found themselves working in boatbuilding, coal and timber delivery and gas supply. Farmers could transport their produce to be sold at much higher prices in London. Wharves and boatyards sprung up around the canal. Boats were hauled by horses, which meant new trade for the town's blacksmiths.

In 1927 the Grand Junction Canal Company was bought by the Regent's Canal Company to form the Grand Union Canal.

James Short, his wife Florence and their family lived in the canal cottage which once stood at Lock 53, next to Lower Kings Road bridge. James, who died in

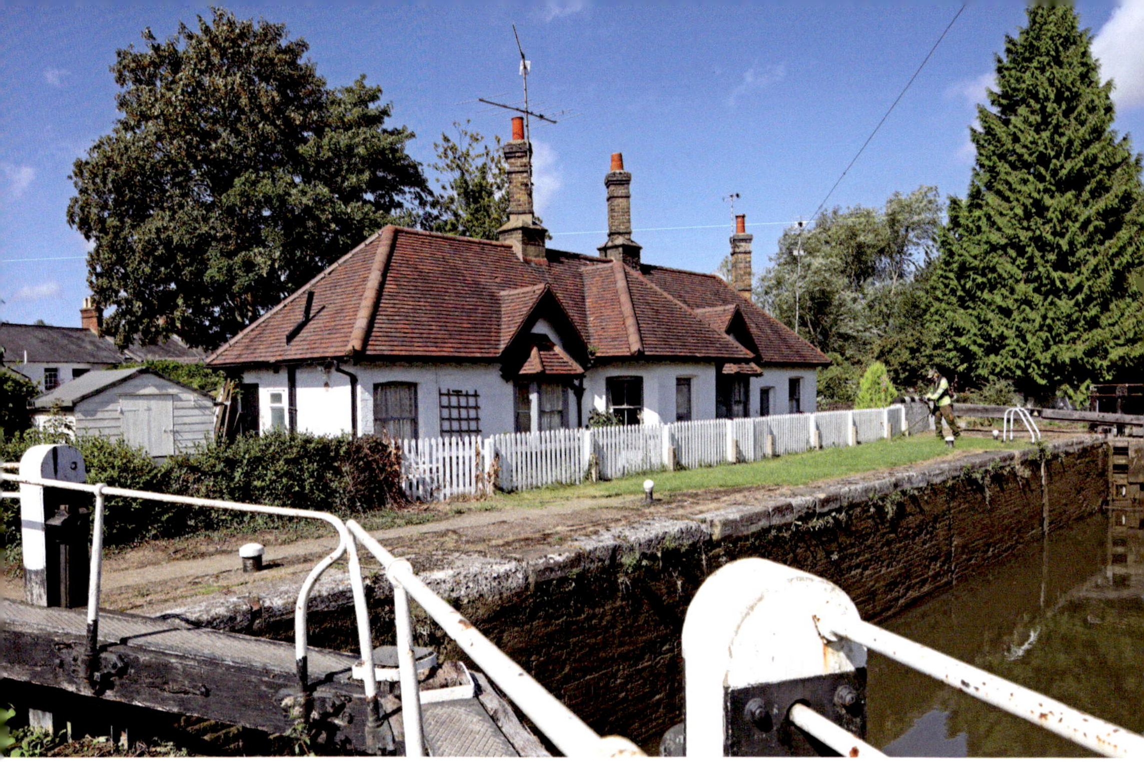

The Grand Union Canal and lock-keeper's cottage.

1951, was a general labourer for the Grand Junction Canal Company. Their son, Wilfred James Short, served in the First World War with the Canadian Pioneers and died of wounds sustained at Ypres in 1916. They are buried in Rectory Lane Cemetery.

## 16. Port of Berkhamsted

Looking upstream, towards Castle Wharf, is the port of Berkhamsted. This was the centre of Berkhamsted's canal trade, navigation and boat-building activities, lying between Raven's Lane and Castle Street.

'The Warehouse', now a family home, once provided stabling for the horses and warehousing facilities on the first floor. Until very recently, this site continued the tradition of boatbuilding in Berkhamsted, which started when the canal arrived.

Peacock and Willetts opened the first boatyard at Castle Wharf in 1799 and launched a boat called *Berkhamsted Castle* in 1801. This was registered in 1802 in the Grand Junction Gauging Register. The boatyard was then run by Costins, followed by Keys and later by Bridgewater Boats.

The once thriving port of Berkhamsted has now lost all its many working wharves, Castle Wharf being not only the last one in Berkhamsted, but the oldest recorded canal boatyard remaining in the south-east of England.

Bridgewater Boats, which designed and built its own hire fleet, was one of several providers of leisure cruises throughout the country. Hire cruising is just one of many sources of revenue needed to meet the massive costs of maintaining our inland waterways. These were the original arteries of our national trade, as essential in the eighteenth and nineteenth centuries as the railways were in the nineteenth and first half of the twentieth centuries, as are our motorways today.

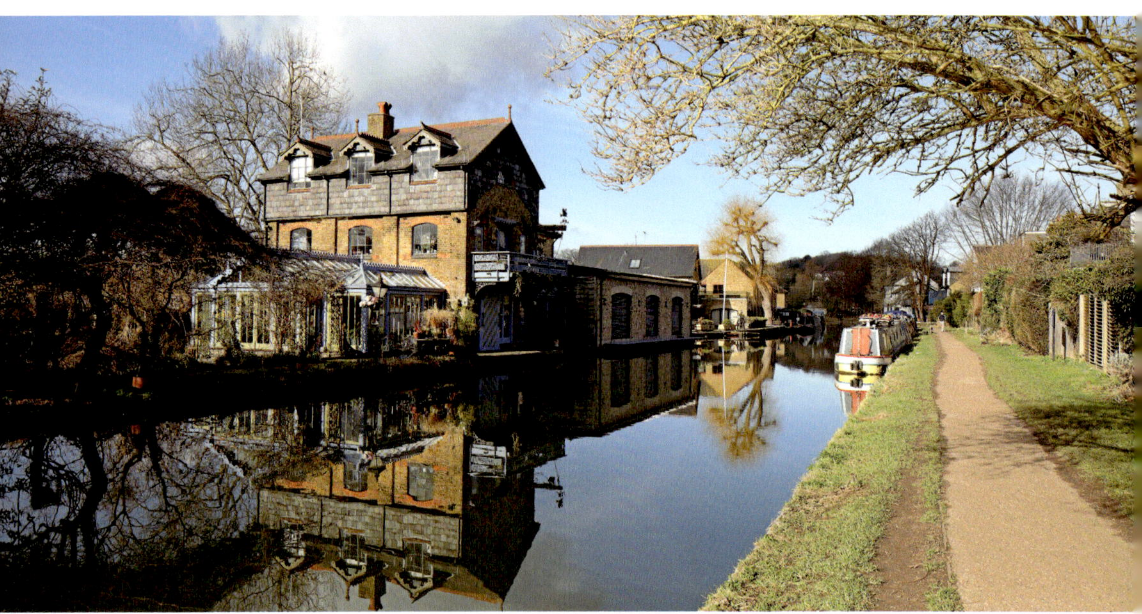

*Above*: The warehouse that overlooks the Grand Union Canal.

*Below*: Once industrial, now residential.

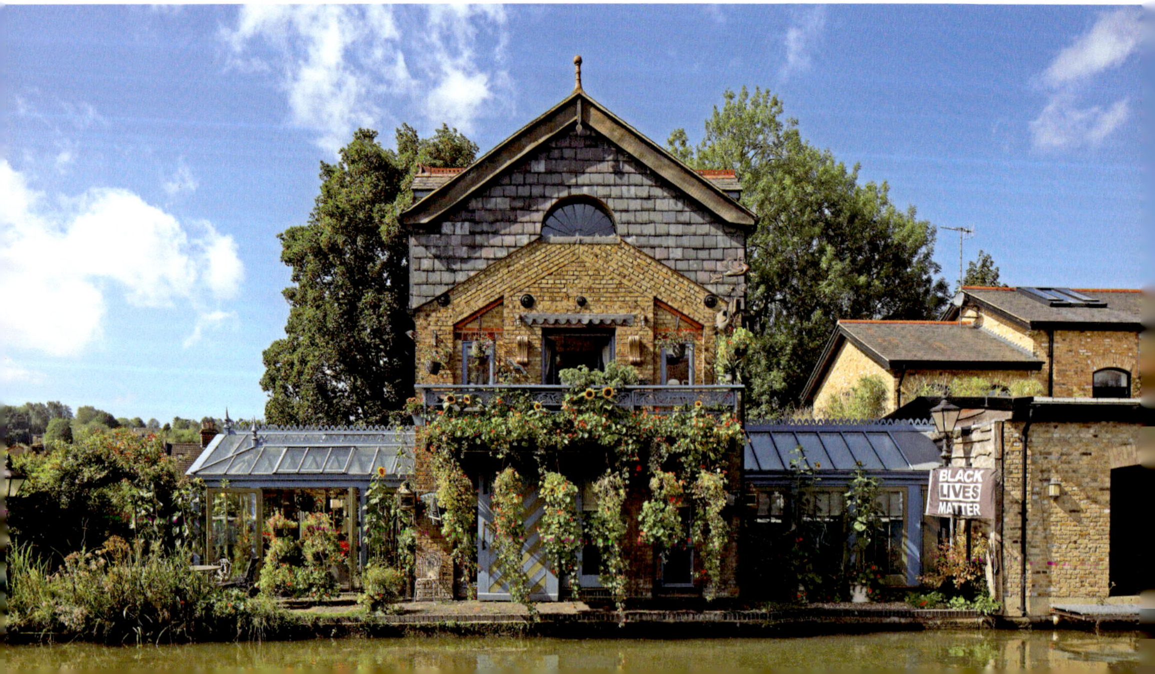

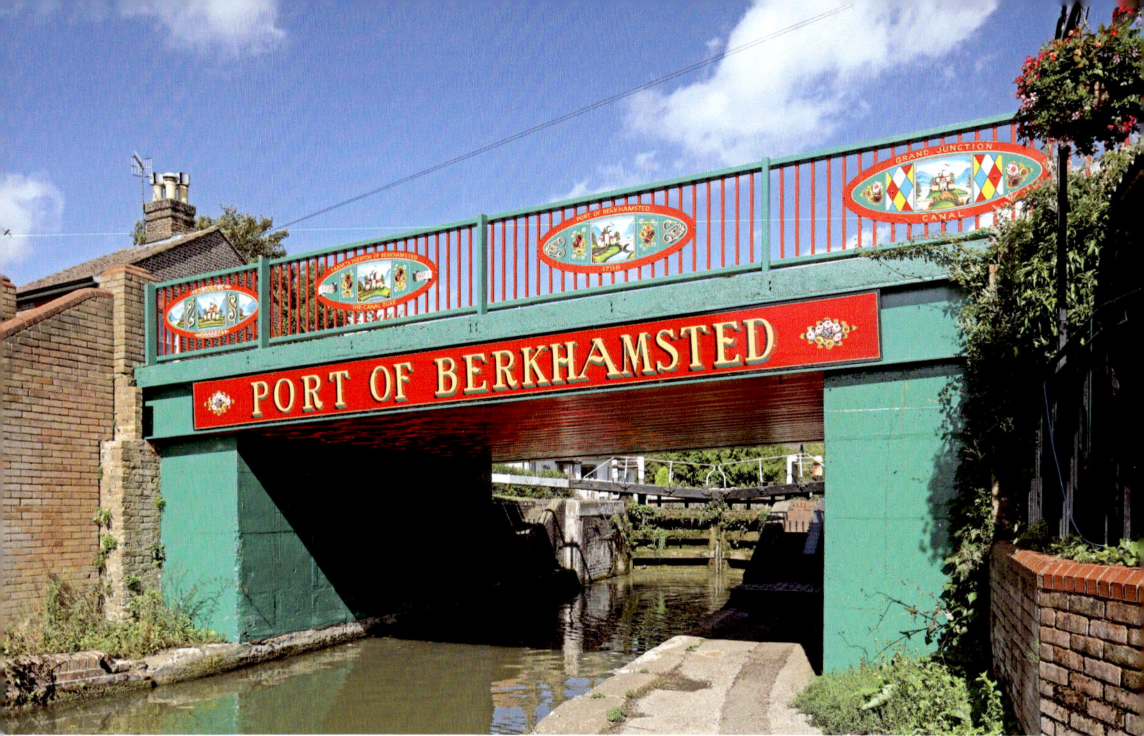


Once the entrance to the Port of Berkhamsted during the canal's heyday.

The Grand Junction Canal Company was formed in 1793 to link the Thames with canals in the Midlands. By 1798 the Grand Junction Canal was open from Brentford all the way through to Berkhamsted, travelling through the Ashridge estate just below the castle. The waterway became fully operational in 1805. The route favoured Berkhamsted as it, in effect, bypassed Hemel Hempstead and made the transportation of corn and timber much easier. The new form of transport meant that, for the first time, coal could be brought into the area in large quantities. Also dung, night soil and street sweepings were brought out of London for use on local farms and on the return journey, hay and straw were sent back to London, thus relieving the roads of heavy wagon traffic. Busy canalside wharves near Castle Street and Ravens Lane enabled domestic and industrial supplies to be delivered by horse-drawn barges or wide-boats (Castle Wharf stood between the river and the canal that are currently occupied by Alsford Wharf and Bridge Court, and at the end of Ravens Lane stands Ravens Wharf).

It was here that canal side taverns also prospered, such as the Castle, the Crooked Billet, the Boat and the Crystal Palace. A boatbuilding timber yard was established between the coal wharves at Castle Street and Ravens Lane.

## 17. The Rising Sun/The Boat/The Crystal Palace

The Rising Sun public house, near the canal lock, lies behind No. 42 George Street (south side). The public house was already built by 1877. The pub is a

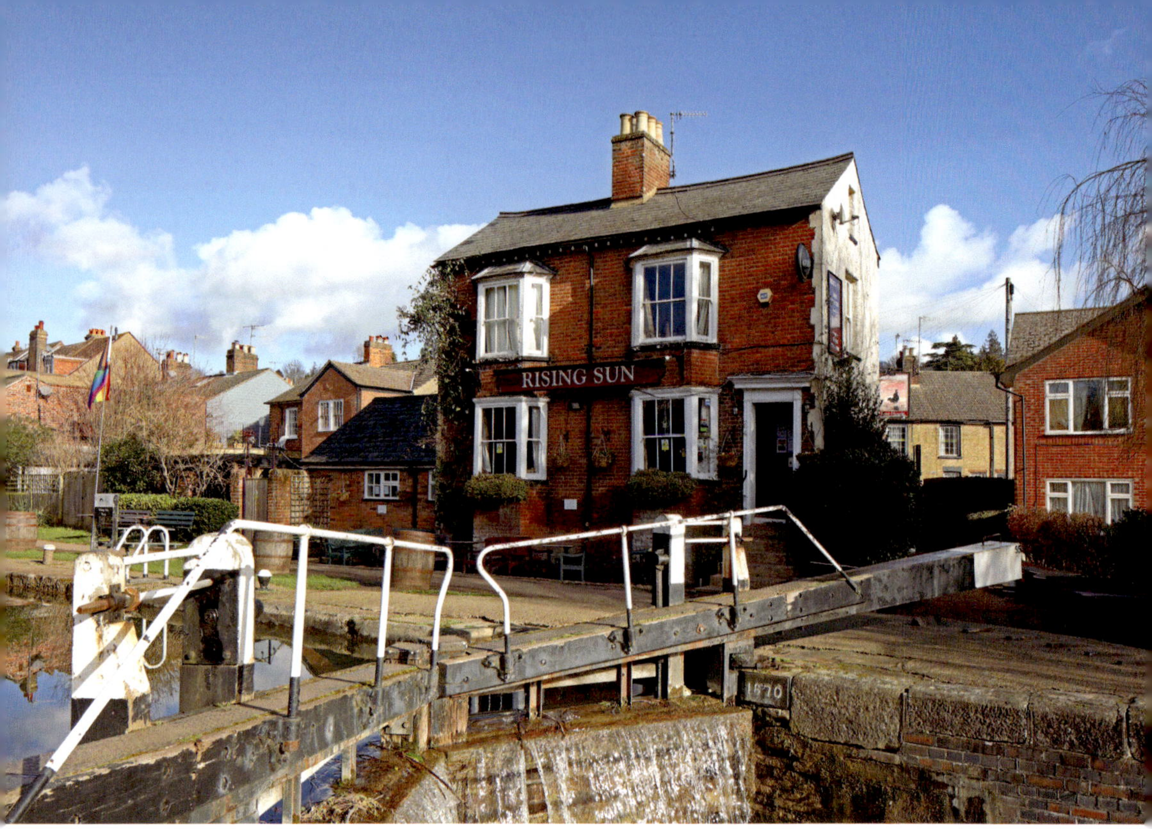

*Above*: The Rising Sun public house.

*Below*: The Boat public house.

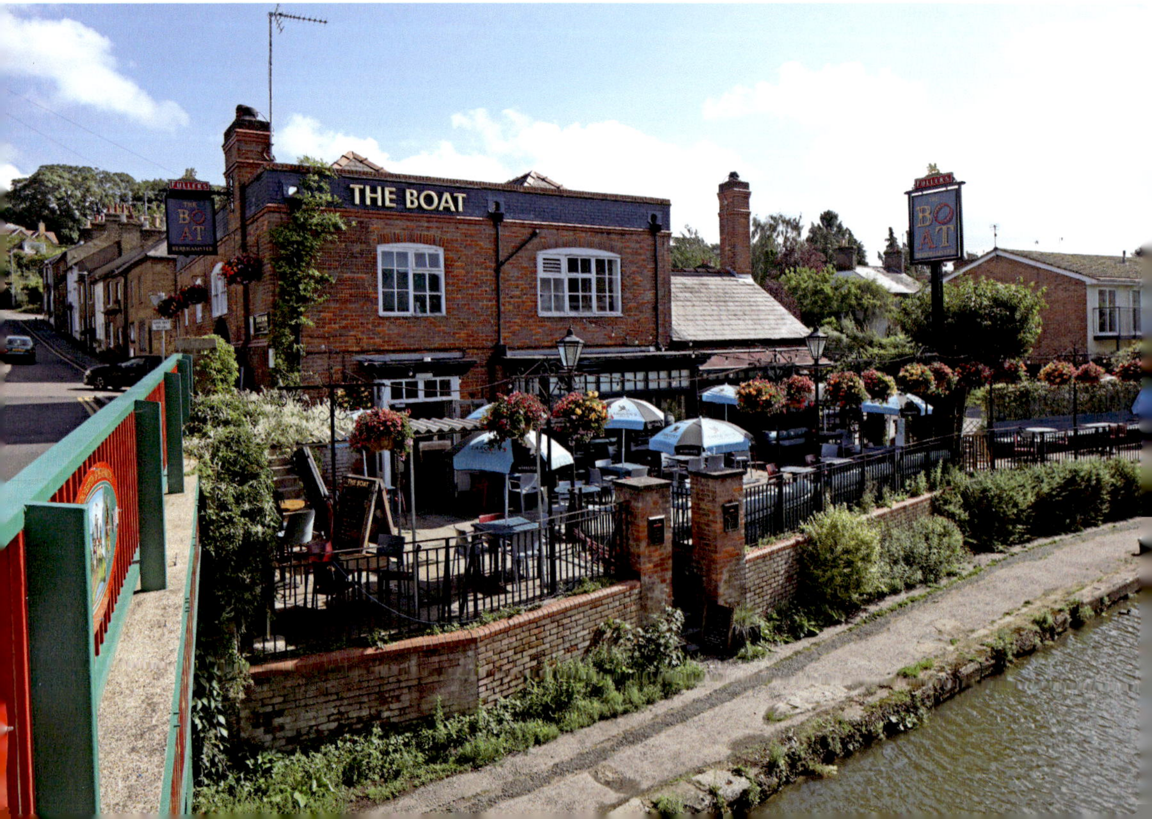

typical alehouse of the mid-1800s with accommodation for the publican's family upstairs. It is the best preserved of the original alehouses next to the canal and its two-storey brick frontage has canted bays that overlook the lock standing nearby. These features and the short access path next to the pub form a picturesque group.

The Boat public house is also landmark structure. It seems to be an old site (an 'inn' in 1877), but the present building is a sympathetic red-brick reconstruction. Steps down from the main level connect with the towpath and the pub has a well-designed terrace overlooking the water.

The rather unusual Crystal Palace public house is probably named after William Paxton, who was Earl Brownlow's land agent and related to Joseph Paxton, the mid-nineteenth-century head gardener from Chatsworth, Derbyshire. His greatest creation, the Crystal Palace, gave its name to this public house at the west end of the sub-district. The pub was used regularly by canal boatmen as the industrial narrowboat trade flourished through Berkhamsted. The building is very distinctive and started life as a small beerhouse in one of two cottages. It was rebuilt in 1854 and much altered in 1867–68.

In Graham Greene's *The Captain and the Enemy*, Greene uses memories of Berkhamsted when the family nursemaids would not take the Greene children for a walk 'along the towing path by the canal' because of the bad language directed at them by the bargees and their children. The Crystal Palace was referred to as the 'Swiss Cottage pub' in *The Captain and the Enemy*, where the Captain refreshed himself.

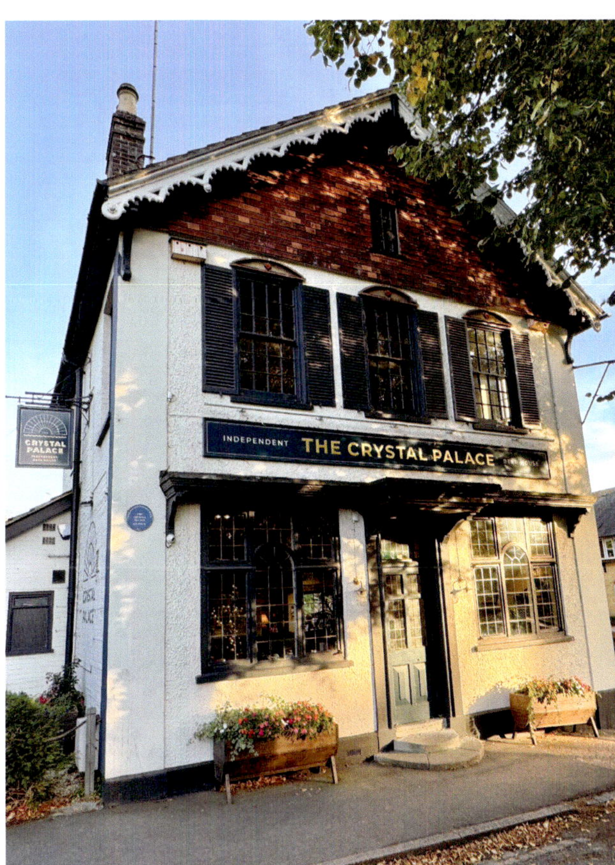


The impressive frontage of the Crystal Palace public house.

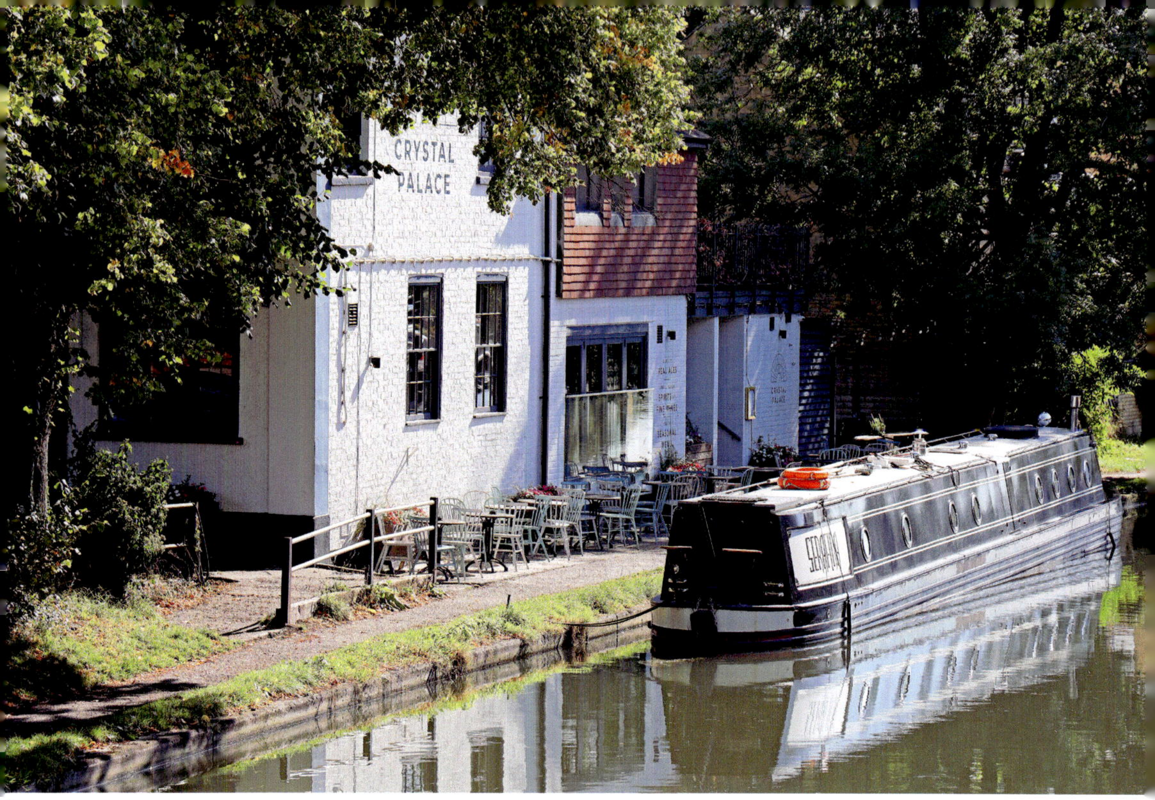

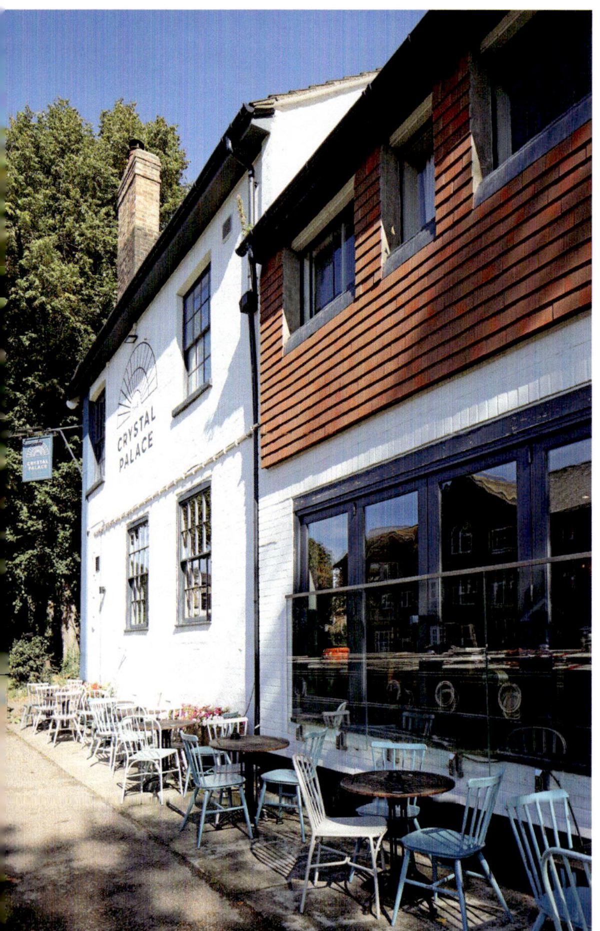

*Above*: A wonderful canal-side setting.

*Left*: The Crystal Palace public house – popular with locals and canal visitors alike.

### 18. Quaker Meeting House

In 1818, upon the removal of Tring Quaker meetings to Berkhamsted, where there had been no meeting before, a meeting house was built that same year on the site of a former gazebo in the garden of Boxwell House, at the time owned by the Quaker Littlejohn family.

The meeting house here is set back from the street frontage behind a dwarf stone wall and a sloping burial ground. The building is rectangular on plan and single storeyed with the entrance front dominated by a large central brick porch with its own separate hipped roof. The porch is an addition of 1964, replacing a much smaller porch. On either side of the porch, the front of the main building has a single round-headed window with small-paned sashes. At the extreme left-hand corner of the front is a cast-iron plaque with the words, 'ERECTED 1818'.

The small burial ground slopes down from the main front of the meeting house to the street. It is enclosed at the sides by a brick wall. Most of the burials apparently date from 1818 to 1885. There are around thirty headstones, which were all moved to line the side walls several years ago.

Within the burial ground is a small apple tree, which was planted in 2018 in celebration of the meeting house's centenary. It is a local variety called Lane's Prince Albert and was developed by Thomas Squires, a local Quaker and also a keen gardener who helped finance this meeting house here in Berkhamsted. He gave a cutting of the tree to nearby Lane's nursery, who named it Lane's Prince Albert after the prince. Queen Victoria had commented on the tree when passing through Berkhamsted to change horses.

The Quaker meeting house.

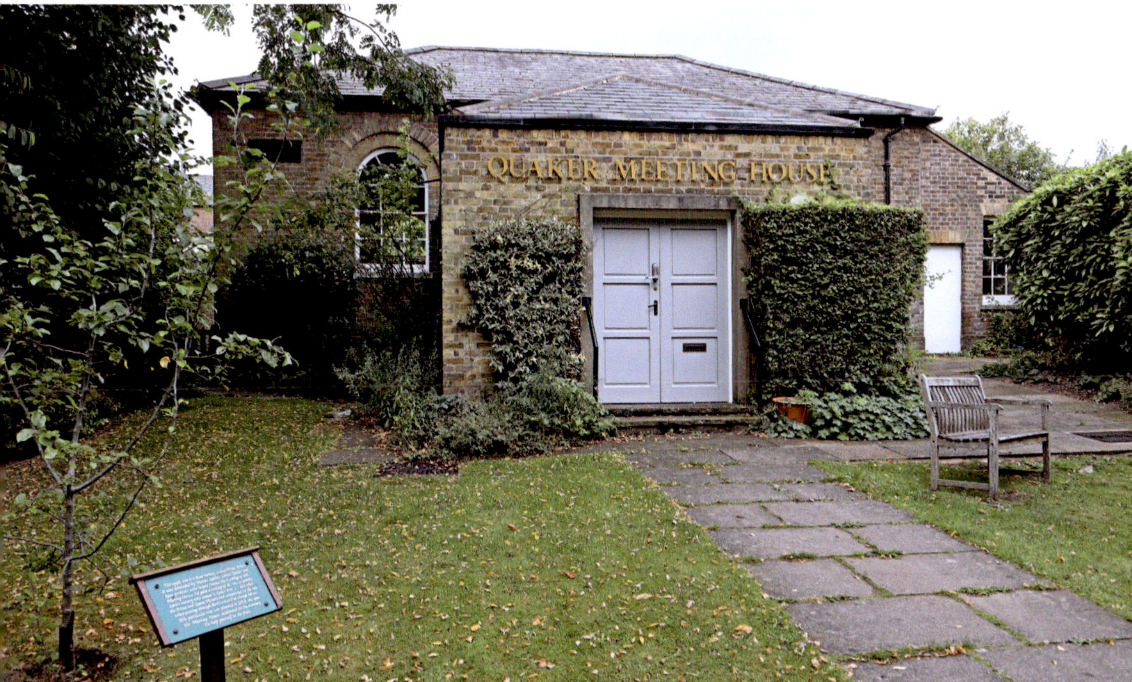

## 19. James Wood & Son

James Wood came to Berkhamsted and established an ironworks business on the High Street in 1826. He lived next door in Monks Cottage. The business was advertised as 'iron fence makers, wire workers & hot water engineers'. After the death of James Wood in 1861, the business was managed by his widow, Fanny.

James Wood & Son continued to trade from these premises for many years as a domestic heating engineers, plumbers and ironmongers. The business later became a plant nursery and garden stores. It still trades under the name of Woods Garden Centre.

The gardening connection with this site also has a long history. The adjacent land was once the site of Lane's Nurseries, a large plant nursery with large greenhouses extending beyond St John's Well Lane and over to the River Bulbourne. It was founded by Henry Lane Sr in 1777 and became highly

*Below left*: James Wood & Son.

*Below right*: Still a popular business in Berkhamsted.

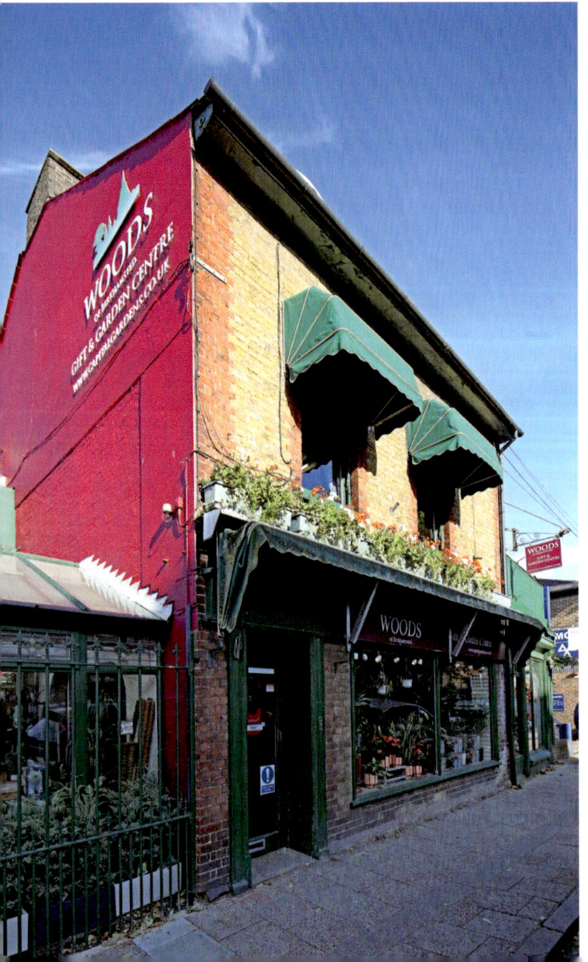


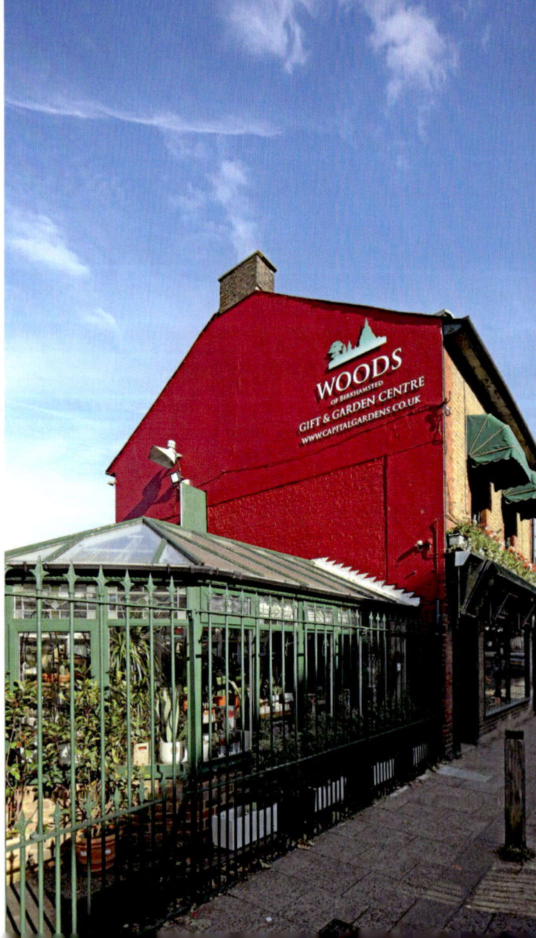

successful, supplying garden plants all over Britain. The family business was managed by a succession of Lanes: Henry's son, also called Henry, took over, succeed in turn by his son, John Edward Lane Sr, and subsequently by John Edward Lane Jr. In 1841, the Lanes promoted a new cultivar of apple (grown by Thomas Squire), the Lane's Prince Albert, named in honour of the visit of Queen Victoria and Prince Albert that year. In the 1850s, Lane's Nurseries also exhibited at the Crystal Palace Exhibition Halls in London and became associated with its architect, Sir Joseph Paxton. John Edward Lane Sr also expanded his business interests into beer brewing and named one of his Berkhamsted pubs after Paxton's marvel, the Crystal Palace.

Three generations of Lanes are buried in nearby Rectory Lane Cemetery, memorials to a family who once dominated Berkhamsted's horticultural and economic landscape.

## 20. The Pightle House

An unusual name for this building is Pightle House, formerly known as Valhalla, when it provided billets for soldiers during the Second World War. Historically, the Pightle was 'the site of a farm-yard with its thrashing-barn, where the sound of the flail aroused the sleepers and gave a friendly call to daily duties'.

Highfield Road used to lead to Highfield House, a mansion that was demolished before the Second World War and the land acquired by the council as part of a housing development. The road was known as the Pightle, a name that is Anglo-Saxon in origin and means 'a strip of meadowland between two copses' or 'small enclosure or close' and was certainly known as this as long ago as the reign of Henry VIII. It has had several official changes of name since then. It was Albert Place in 1841 and Prospect Street in 1851 before eventually becoming Highfield Road. Pightle House is a handsome old building and a reminder of its once unusual name.

Next door to Pightle House is the former Queen's Arms, which was an inn on the corner of Berkhamsted High Street and Highfield Road. Records going back centuries name a succession of landlords, including Francis Barker in 1607, John Waller in 1839 and Alfred Shead in 1897. Pightle House next door was once joined to the pub.

In 1871, the Heading family were recorded as living at the Queen's Arms, and William Henry Heading Sr was the licensed victualler here. He died in 1878 and was buried in the family plot in Rectory Lane Cemetery. The Queen's Arms closed as a public house in 1968, but it can still be seen today, though is now a private house. It is a traditional seventeenth-century timber-framed building with a distinctive narrow corner door.

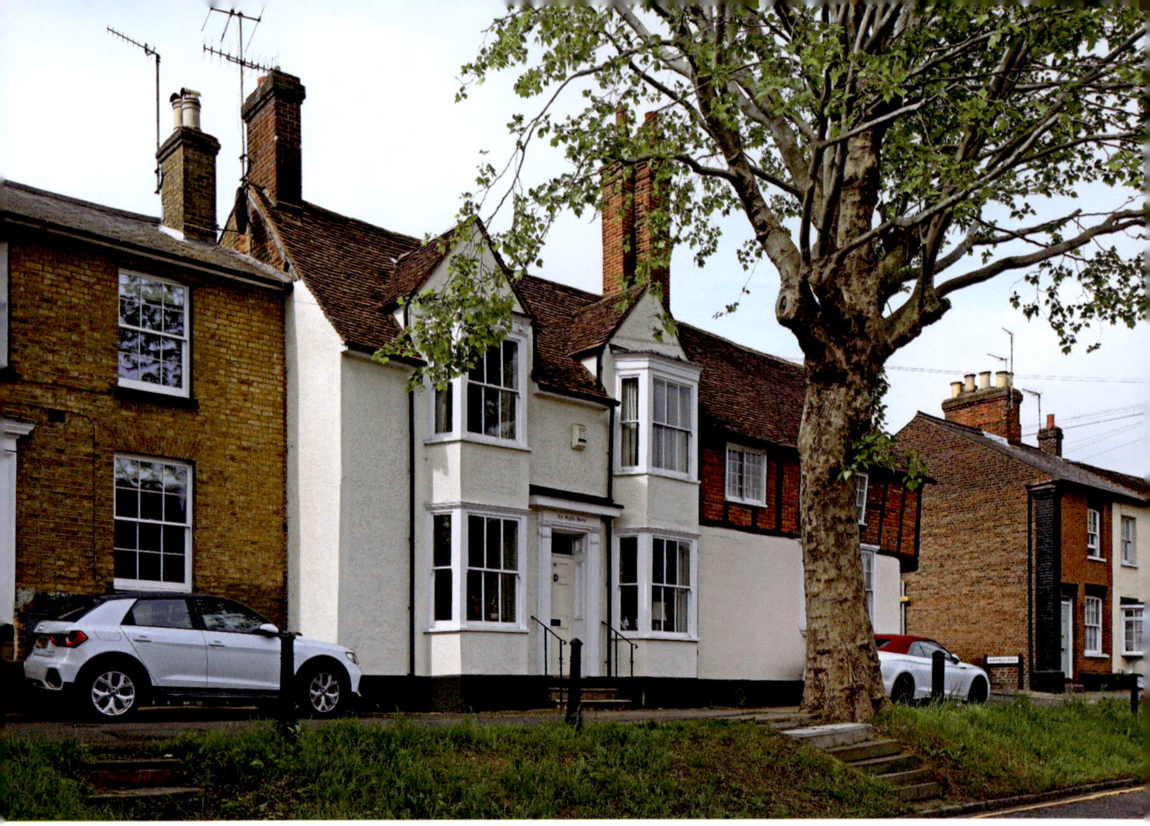

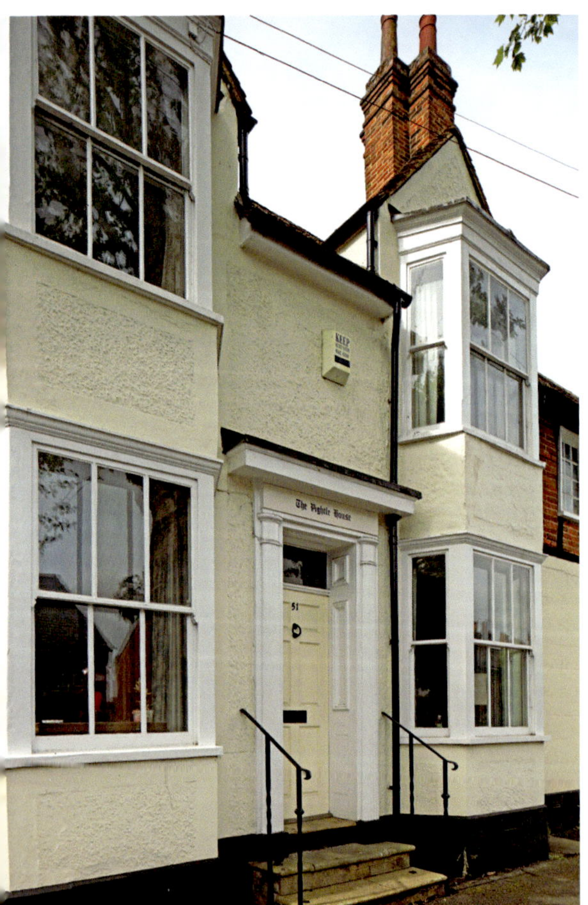

*Above and left*: The unusually named Pightle House.

## 21. The Poplars

The Poplars is one of a number of substantial nineteenth-century middle-class houses along the High Street, of which only a few have remained residential. It takes its name from tall Lombardy poplars which used to line this part of the High Street. The actor Sir Michael Horden was born here in 1911. It was also the home of William Cooper.

William Cooper, the founder of Cooper's in Berkhamsted, was a young farrier born in the little village of Clunbury, Shropshire. He arrived in Berkhamsted by carrier in around 1842 with very few possessions and his pestle and mortar. By the time of his death in 1885 he was a wealthy man with a flourishing business, which was to continue to expand until its final demise at the end of the twentieth century. William was one of the first to qualify as a vet at the newly formed Royal College of Veterinary Surgeons and gradually became accepted by the local farming community.

His real interest, however, was in developing an effective powder-based cure for sheep scab, the principal ingredient of which was arsenic. This he began to produce at his chemical works in Ravens Lane in the mid-1850s, gradually acquiring more land as his business expanded. He ran his own printing department, the Clunbury Press, built houses for senior workers and members of his family (Sibdon Place and Clunbury House). William and Mary Cooper had no children, so as he grew older William brought three of his nephews into the business and the firm became William Cooper & Nephews.

The Poplars.

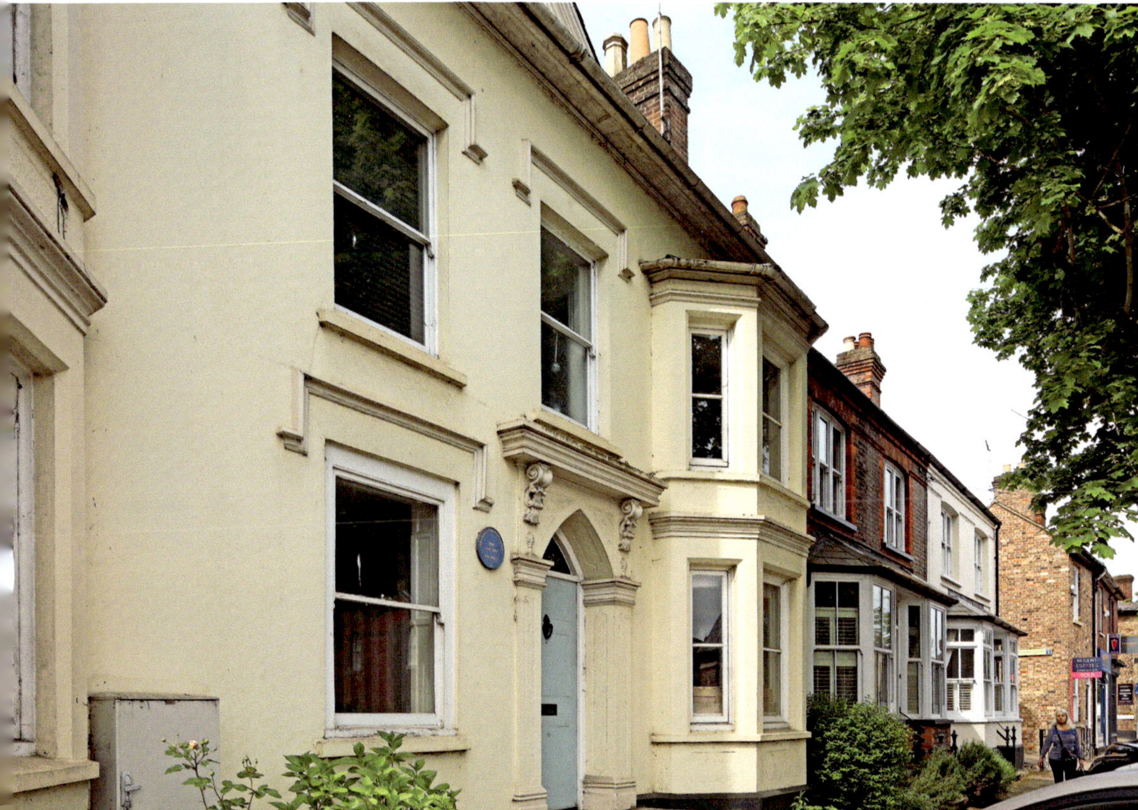

## 22. The Red House

John Tawell, a prominent local citizen and benefactor, lived in the Red House. At sixty-one, he and his wife, Sarah, shared a 'Quaker-lifestyle' of outwardly respectable disposition. They lived here in Berkhamsted and could often be seen in town. However, both had been expelled from the movement on their marriage. John Tawell was so righteous he might have been regarded as above the law.

But he was not above the law, and though his earlier standing as a Quaker probably saved him from the gallows when he was a young man, a quarter of a century later he would hang for the cold-blooded murder, by poisoning, of his secret mistress, thirty-year-old Sarah Hart. On 28 March 1845, he was hanged at Aylesbury before a crowd of over 2,000, but not before he wrote down a full confession to the crime of murdering Sarah Hart, and how he had tried to kill her the previous September. Until that time his wife remained loyal, refusing to believe her husband was a murderer.

As for Tawell, his hanging was 'botched'. He was of slight build and the hangman did not allow sufficient 'drop'; instead of Tawell's neck breaking, he took 10 minutes to slowly strangle to death.

Tawell was also the first person to be arrested as the result of telecommunications technology. A man in distinctive Quaker dark clothing had been observed to leave

The Red House.

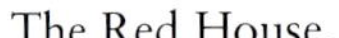

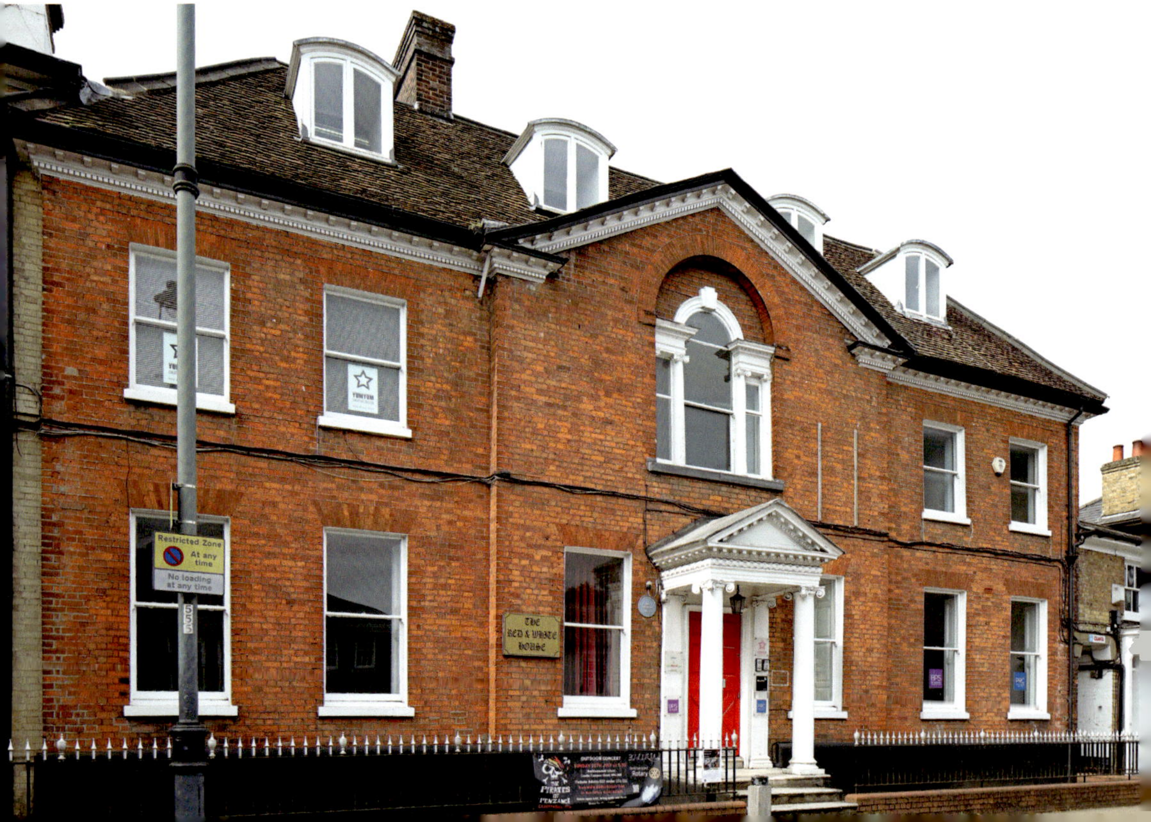

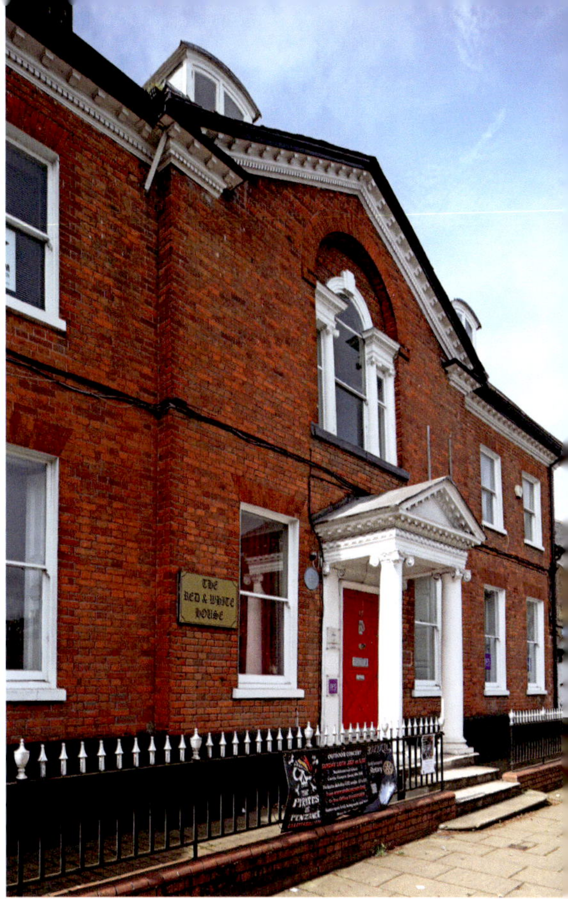

The Red House has a macabre history.

Sarah's house shortly before she died. Following his trail, the police found that a person answering his description had caught the train at Slough, heading for Paddington station in London. The police immediately used the newly installed telegraph to send a message to Paddington, giving the particulars, and desiring his capture. 'He is in the garb of a kwaker,' ran the message, 'with a brown coat on, which reaches nearly to his feet.' There was no 'Q' in the alphabet of the two-needle instrument, and the clerk at Slough therefore spelt the word 'Quaker' with a 'kwa'. 'Kwaker' was eventually understood, but only after several requests to repeat.

Having earned its place in history, the electro-magnetic telegraph used to entrap him was put on show to the public at a shilling a head.

## 23. The Dower House

A former manor house was located close to the town centre. Pilkington Manor was home to some of the town's wealthiest families during the nineteenth century. The name 'Pilkington' is mentioned in a local survey dated 1616. The estate, established around this old manorial site, at one time stretched from the High Street to White Hill and from Castle Street to Ravens Lane. The manor house

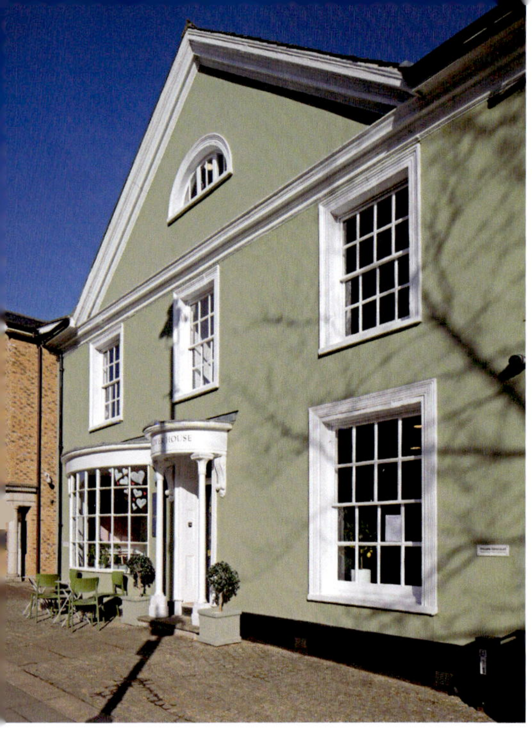

The Dower House.

survived into the twentieth century and was built in the eighteenth century. In 1775, the house together with outbuildings, gardens, fishponds and 13½ acres of meadowland were let to Samuel Simmons on a fourteen-year lease. At this time, it was a house of such significant importance that a pew and vault were reserved at St Peter's Church for whoever was living at Pilkington Manor.

Early in the nineteenth century, ownership of the estate passed from a London brewer named Joseph Kirkman to Charles Gordon, who made his fortune in Jamaica at the height of the slave trade. The house by now was impressive and had a large walled garden, stretching as far as the marsh in the valley where there was also a large ornamental lake suitable for boating. When Gordon died in 1829, Pilkington Manor was bought by Frederick Miller, who had decided to take a profit on his investment and sell off a large part of the estate by 1852. The land was then made available for residential development as well as provided the site for the original Cooper's factory works. Some of the land was also used as a graveyard for the large Congregational Church on the corner of Chapel Street, of which Mr Miller became a substantial benefactor. The elegant house known as the Dower House is said to be the former dower house of Pilkington Manor. The old manor house was demolished in 1959 and the site has since been redeveloped to provide a row of modern shops.

## 24. Brownlow House

This red-brick building on the corner of Ravens Lane and Chapel Street was once the Brownlow Arms pub. The building does not appear on 1839 maps, so it was probably built c. 1859, and possibly by its first owner, the noted Berkhamsted entrepreneur John Edward Lane Sr (1808–89). The bar was kept by Thomas Morgan. A small cluster of pubs sprang up in this part of town in the mid-nineteenth century, reflecting the shift of demand from the High Street coaching inns to the new footfall generated by the construction of the railway station.

The pub is named after the local landowner at Ashridge, John Egerton-Cust, Lord Brownlow. His agent, William Paxton (nephew of Joseph Paxton), lived nearby, and was associated with Lane.

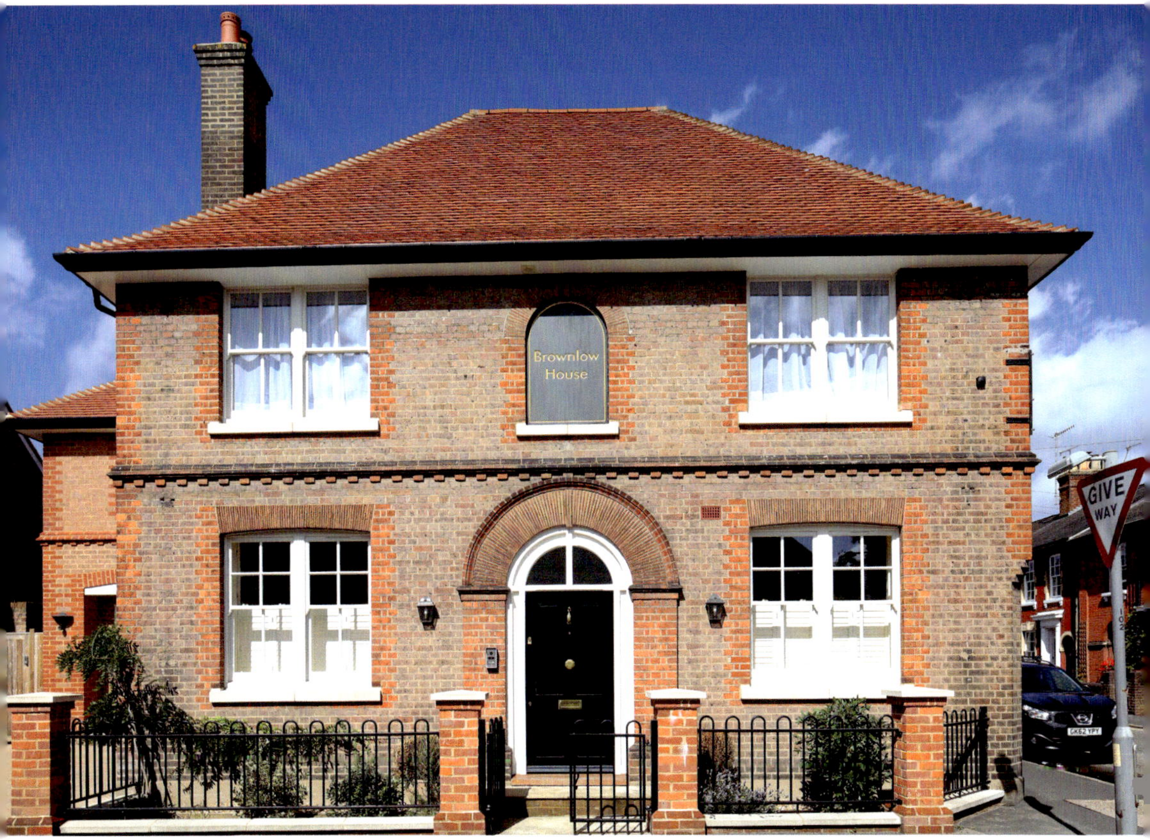

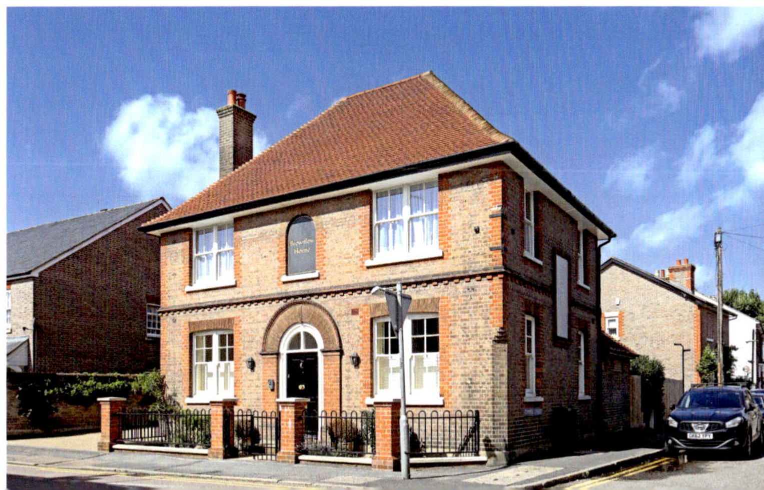

*Above and right*:
Brownlow House, a
former public house.

Lane owned the Brownlow Arms until 1871, when he sold it, along with the Swan and the George, to Henry James Foster. Lane died in 1889 and was buried in Rectory Lane Cemetery.

The Brownlow Arms was later acquired by the Aylesbury Brewery. In more recent times it was in use as offices and is now a private house.


## 25. Berkhamsted Town Hall

One of the most prominent buildings on the High Street is the highly ornate Berkhamsted Town Hall. It was built in 1859–60 for the Berkhamsted Parish Council and designed in the Gothic Revival style by renowned architect Edward Buckton Lamb (1806–69). The building was wholly funded by public subscription. Buckton's design is magnificent and features an octagonal turret and spire, tall lancet windows, intricate Gothic ornamentation and a projecting clock over the High Street.

This new building replaced the Old Court House adjacent to St Peter's Church, which still exists and provided new meeting chambers for the council as well as a magistrates' court. It also contained a market hall on the ground floor, which replaced the Tudor market hall which had once been located on the High Street but had burnt down in 1854. Many local figures of note had supported the creation of a new Town Hall.

The official opening of the Town Hall took place on 22 August 1860. The *Bucks Herald* of 22 August 1860 reported:

> The new Town Hall at Berkhampstead [*sic*] – in the old English style of architecture – was opened in due form. It is a large and well-lighted room, built by Messrs. Matthews and Nash and designed by Mr. Lamb, the architect. This being the first public meeting held within the walls, we have the pleasure of stating that for light, sound, &c., it has fully answered the expectations of those interested in the undertaking.

Berkhamsted Town Hall was also where the Berkhamsted Mechanics' Institute was located, an educational establishment for working men that was fervently supported by Revd Hutchinson's successor in the parish, Revd John Wolstenholme Cobb (1829–83). In 1890, the Town Hall was extended at the rear to provide further accommodation for the Mechanics' Institute.

In 1898, the Berkhamsted Urban District Council (UDC) was established and consequently required new premises. In 1938, a new Civic Centre was opened on the opposite side of the High Street, signifying a change in the town's municipal history. The Old Town Hall remained in use as a venue for public functions. Unfortunately, in the 1970s the building became derelict and was under the threat of demolition, as it was deemed economically unviable. A local campaign to save the building was led by former town mayor John Cook, who won support from local celebrities including authors Graham Greene, Richard Mabey and composer Antony Hopkins. Thankfully, common sense prevailed, and the Old Town Hall was saved from destruction and restored.

By the 1980s and 1990s the ground-floor market hall became a small shopping arcade with a variety of restaurants and independent craft shops, known as the Making Place (later renamed re:create), with a walkway through to a public garden at the rear. Eventually the arcade was closed and converted into a single space which, over recent years, has been let to a series of restaurant businesses including Caffé Uno, Brasserie Chez Gérard, Carluccios, and the Copper House. The Old Town Hall is without question one of the town's finest architectural assets. It is worthy of its Grade II listing and continues to offer a venue for public events, craft fairs and weddings.

The building's architect, Edward Buckton Lamb, later went on to work for Prime Minister Benjamin Disraeli, remodelling Hughenden Manor in Buckinghamshire. He died nine years after his Berkhamsted masterpiece was completed and was buried on the western side of Highgate Cemetery in London.

The Town Hall's usage as a place to dine is reflected in a menu card of a dinner given here in 1896 to employees of Cooper's chemical works. It included roast beef, roast turkey, roast veal, boiled ham, sucking pigs, boiled mutton and caper sauce, roast pork, roast mutton, boiled chickens and white sauce, roast chickens, boiled beef, plum pudding, rhubarb tarts, apple tarts, mince pies, blancmange, tipsy cakes, jellies, cheese, celery and dessert. It was noted at the time that while the Town Hall diners were enjoying a sumptuous repast, scores of families in Berkhamsted were hungry. It was not for nothing that free soup

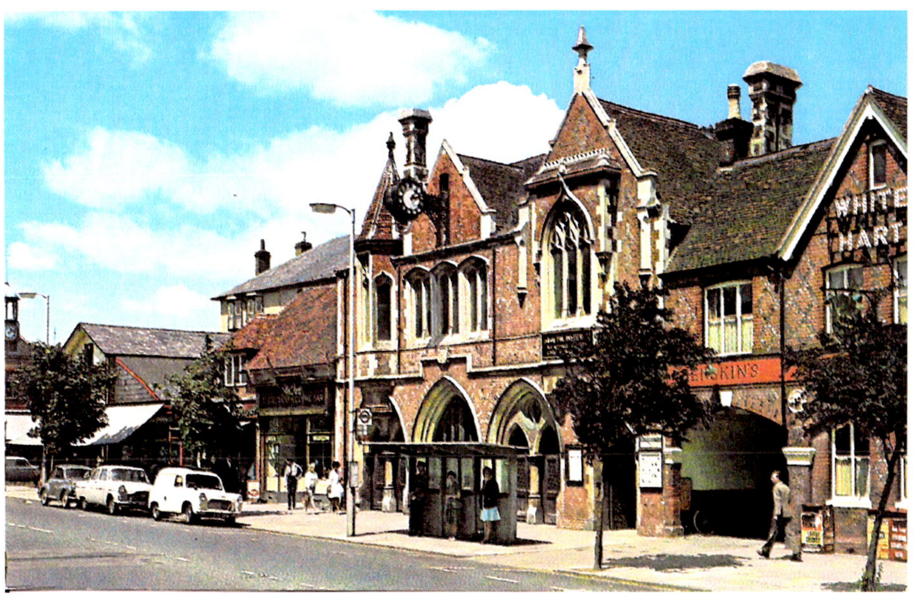


The Town Hall in the 1960s or early 1970s.

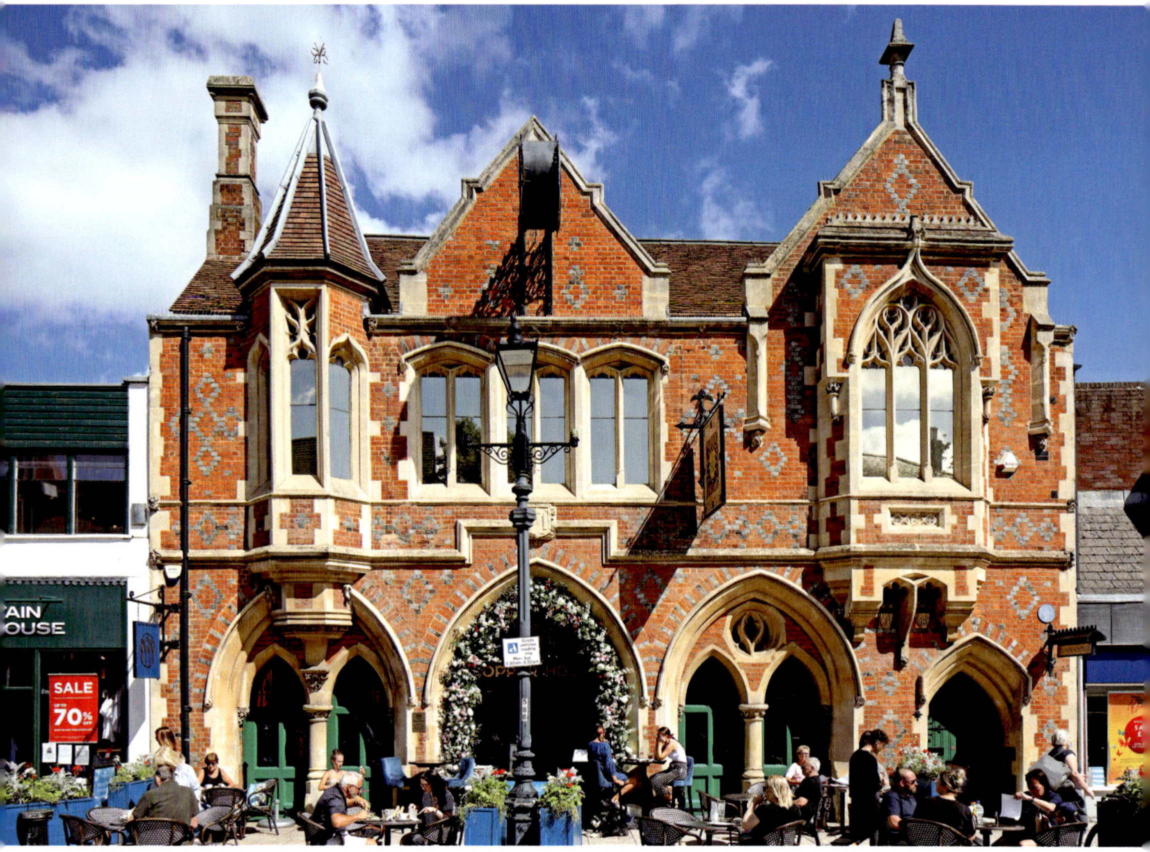

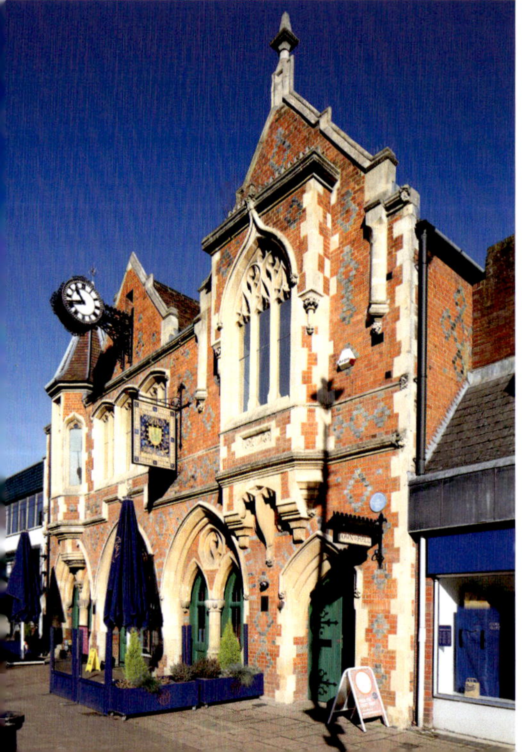

*Above*: The former Town Hall, now catering for visitors' culinary needs rather than municipal requirements.

*Left*: One of the most prominent buildings on the High Street.

kitchens were set up in the castle grounds and at Foster's Brewery. It should not be forgotten that despite the affluence of the town in the twenty-first century, there was dire poverty in Victorian Berkhamsted, especially in the winter months, and malnutrition was widespread despite the well-stocked shops in the town.

## 26. Sibdon Place

Beyond the Baptist Church to the west lies Sibdon Place, a very fine row of Victorian villas. It stands on the corner of the High Street and Ravens Lane (Nos 66–74), and is an attractive small group of terraced houses built in red brick with terracotta decorative detailing and yellow-brick banding/headers. Common features of these houses include bay windows, sash windows with segmental heads, projecting stone sills, doorcases, panelled doors, fanlights and finials. They are wonderfully preserved. Set slightly back from the pavement with low brick front walls and small planted gardens, their original metal railings that stood on the wall have long since been removed. The adjoining red-brick Victorian property with prominent chimney stacks, whose gable is dated 1863 in blue brick (Nos 76 and 78 High Street), is the tallest commercial building at the east end of the High Street and marks the beginning of the town centre that extends from Manor Street onwards.

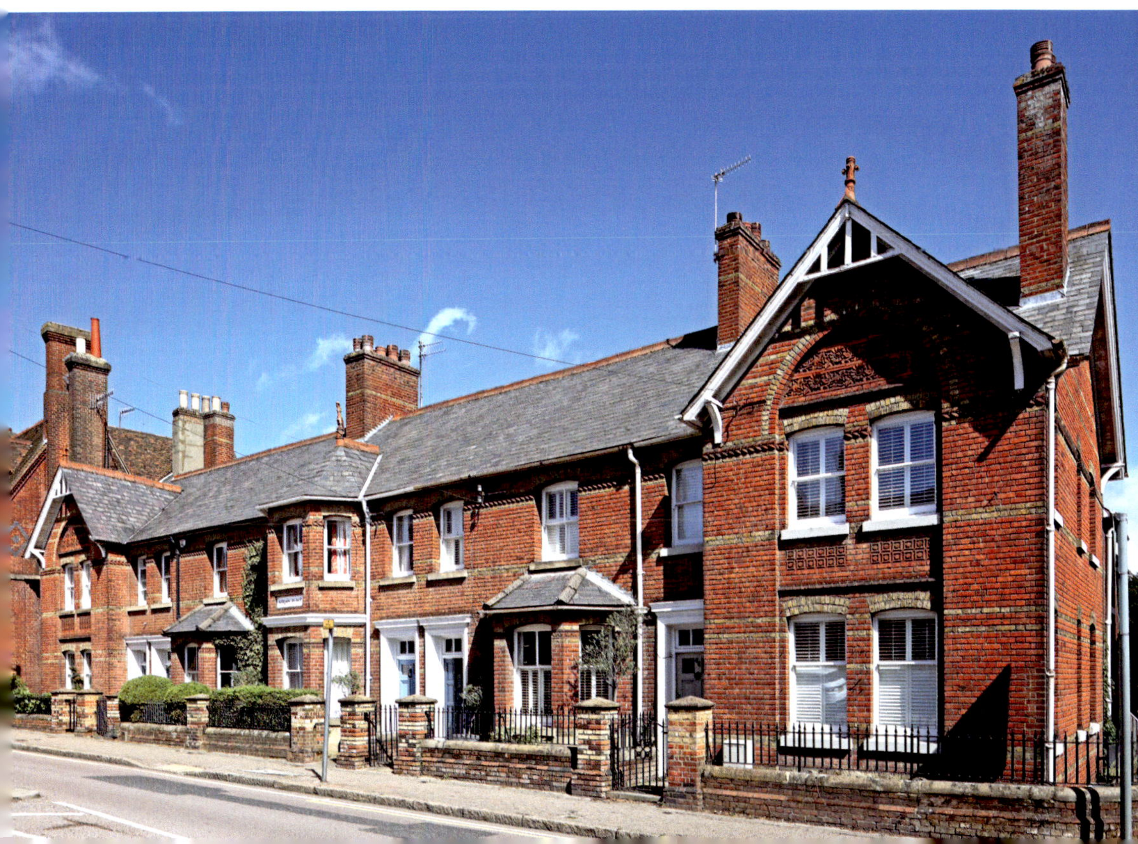

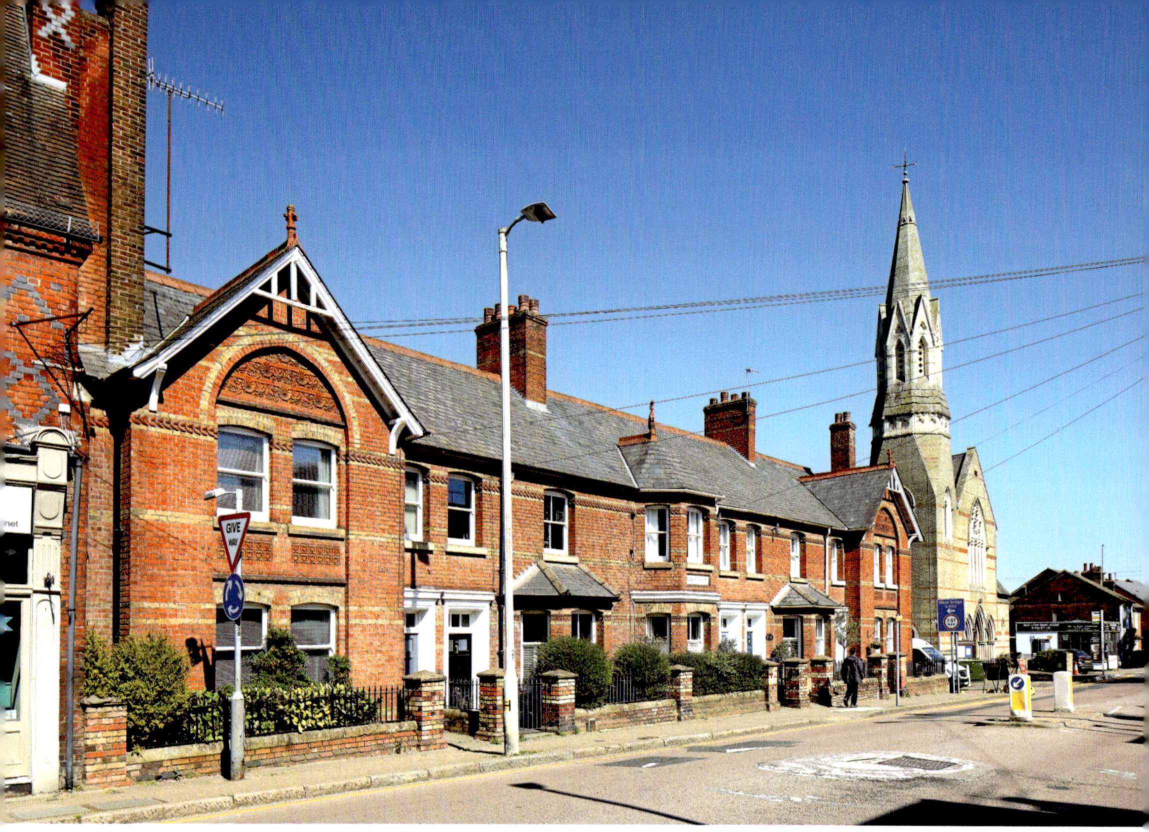

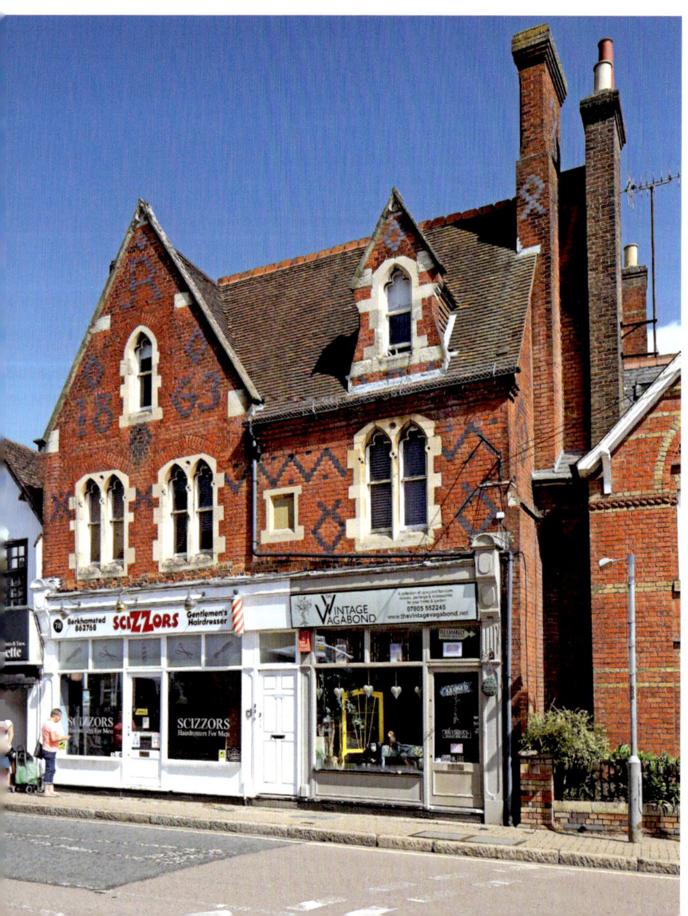

*Previous and above*: Sibdon Place, a fine row of Victorian residences.

*Left*: The date of the building is very clear.

## 27. Berkhamsted Baptist Church

The Berkhamsted Baptist Church dates from at least 1640 and is amongst the oldest in the denomination. A representative of the church attended the General Baptist Assemblies held in London in 1654 and 1656, and by 1676 the congregation had at least 100 members.

Thomas Monk, one of the founding members of Berkhamsted Baptist Church, was arrested in 1640 for 'contemptuously absenting himself from parish church worship' and for 'failing to baptise his four children'. The magistrates delivered the draconian sentence of death to Monk and nine other men and two women. Only the intervention of King Charles II prevented the sentence being carried out and Thomas Monk was released to continue his fruitful ministry. From their early beginnings Baptists were Nonconformists, believing in religious freedom and serving their local communities in the name of Jesus Christ.

Nearly 400 years later, Berkhamsted Baptist Church continues to serve the local community, from its base in the High Street, but its history is a long one.

The congregation was not an isolated one. In its early years the church was strongly associated with the Chesham Baptists and was part of a wider Buckinghamshire Association. Separate churches at Tring and Redbourn established in the seventeenth century were apparently offshoots of the Berkhamsted/Chesham association, which from 1712 onwards was also supporting preaching stations at

Berkhamsted Baptist Church.

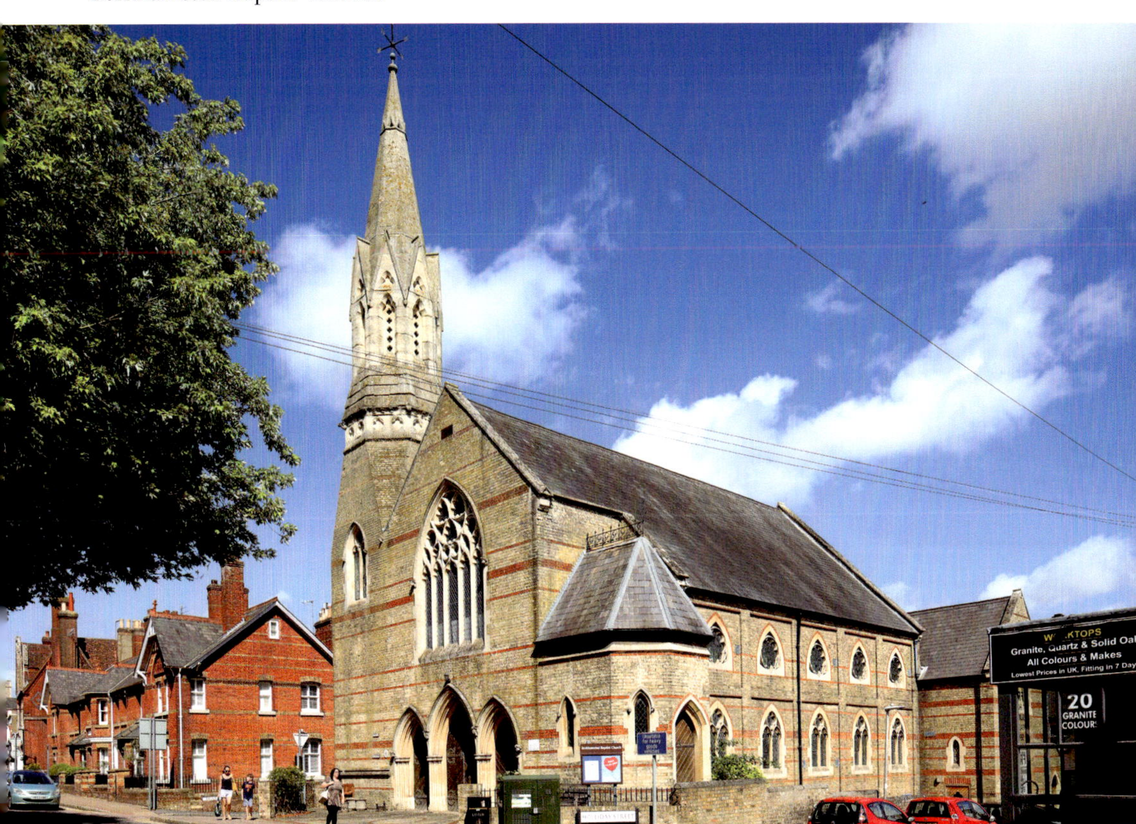

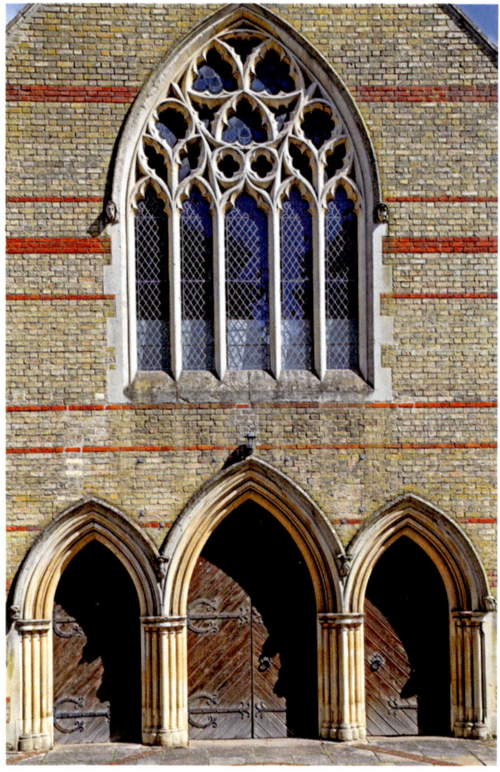

The architecturally beautiful frontage of the Baptist Church.

Colney Street, Bedmond, Bovingdon, Frithsden and Hudnall in Hertfordshire and Whelply Hill, Pipers Hill, Chartridge (from 1720) and Wendover (from 1788) in Buckinghamshire. By 1750 the dual Berkhamsted/Chesham Church was enlarged by association with a further congregation at Frogmore End, Tring.

In 1809 the Berkhamsted Baptist Church joined the recently established New Connexion of General Baptists and subsequently became part of the Hertfordshire Union (established 1810), predecessor of the Hertfordshire Baptist Association.

Until 1722 the Berkhamsted Baptists held their meetings on the private properties of members. In 1722, however, a site in Water Lane, Berkhamsted, was purchased and a meeting house built which, later enlarged, remained in use until 1864 when it was demolished and a new chapel built in the High Street. A chapel was also erected by the Berkhamsted Baptists at Frithsden in 1834 for the use of members who had been meeting in that hamlet since at least 1798, but this was closed for services in the 1930s.

## 28. The Goat Public House

The Goat is a nineteenth-century public house on the site of an old thatched inn. Here, drovers used to stay while their cattle were pounded in the three 'closes' that gave their name to the lane by the side of the Rex. Berkhamsted Local History

& Museum Society have studied the history of many of the taverns in the town. Many had notorious reputations.

At the top of Highfield Road stood the Chaffcutter's Arms, where in 1824 Joseph Howard catered for the thirsts of farm labourers. A favourite resort of businessmen was the Five Bells, which was also the haunt of bare-fisted fighters. A few doors away stood the Red Lion, which ceased to be an inn in 1870. Circuses were often held behind the pub towards Butts Meadow. Adjoining the Sayer almshouses was a tiny alehouse, the Royal Oak. Opposite was the Star and Garter. Shortly after the First World War, Berkhamsted lost three more licensed houses: the Stag (at Gossoms End), the seventeenth-century Boot in Castle Street and the Edward VI (originally the Henry VIII) in Mill Street. Northchurch also lost its old Pheasant Inn.

One of the most interesting is the Kings Arms, which was at the height of its fame in the coaching days. Trustees of a church charity held their meetings at the Swan. The One Bell, built on the village green next door to the long-vanished market house, was a popular resort of stallholders and their customers. The Fish, in Mill Street, was well patronised by waggoners in days when grain was taken to the old water mill.

In 1824, John Siret, landlord of the Goat, made a speciality of catering for drovers. The Cow Roast (or Cow Rest) also catered for drovers. The Crooked Billet was referenced in the session rolls for 1753 when a shovel-maker and a

The Goat public house.

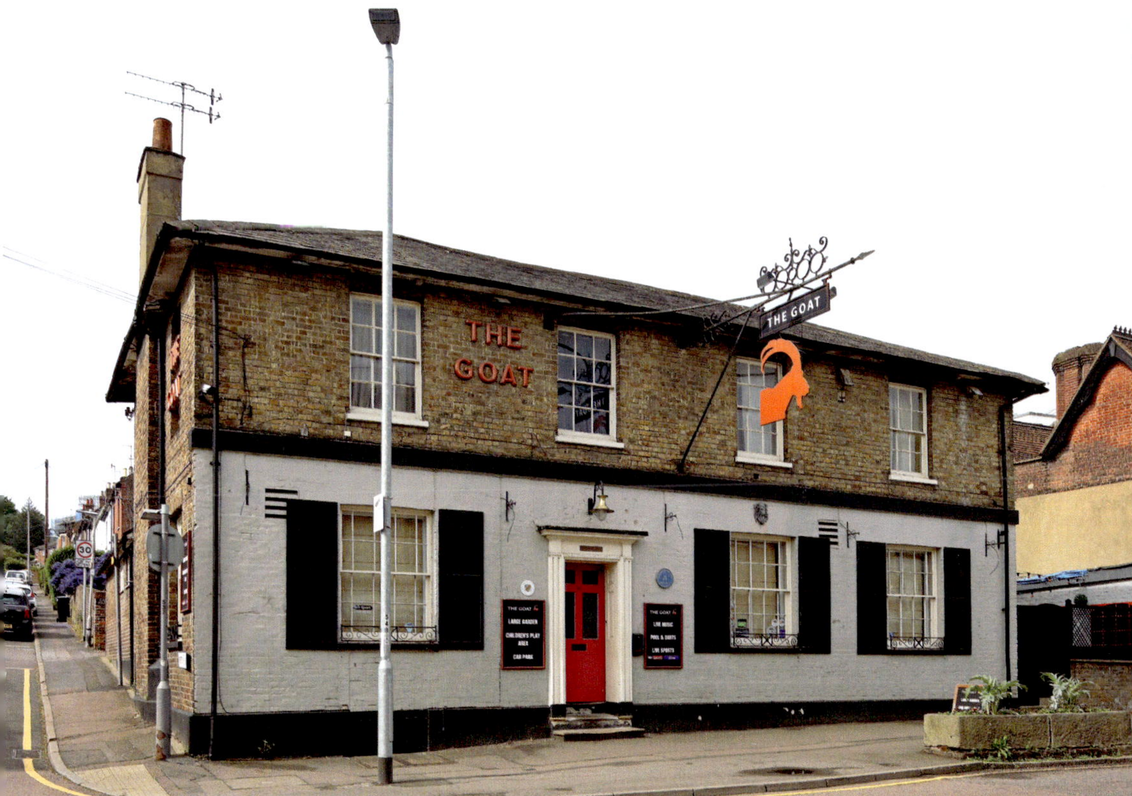

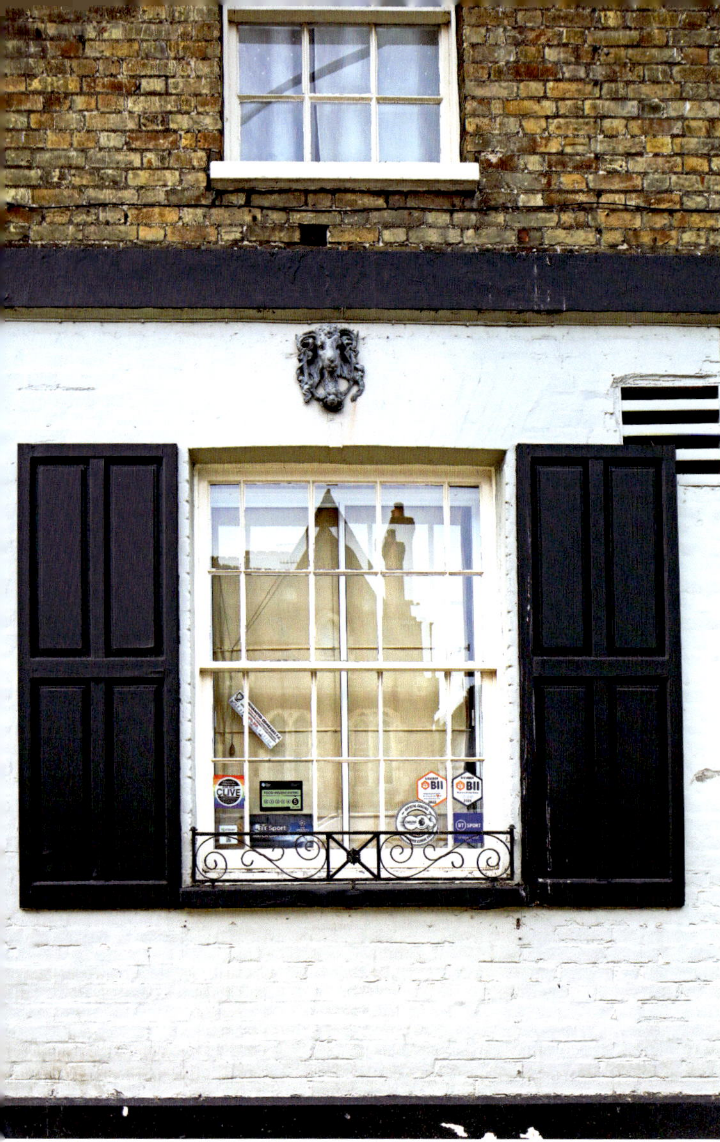

A goat watching the world go by.

spoon-maker were in a dispute over the sale of an empty sack for sixpence and a pint of beer. Closing time was remarkably early: 9 p.m. from Easter to Michaelmas and 8 p.m. during the rest of the year.

## 29. Former Gardener's Arms

Prominent on the corner of Chapel Street is a pair of mid-nineteenth-century houses which were originally built as alehouses, one being the former Gardener's Arms, but first used as shops. Henry Nash, a local historian and benefactor, lived here. Nash had a strong interest in education and helped establish Berkhamsted School for Girls as well as Berkhamsted Mechanics' Institute, early meetings of which were held in this house.

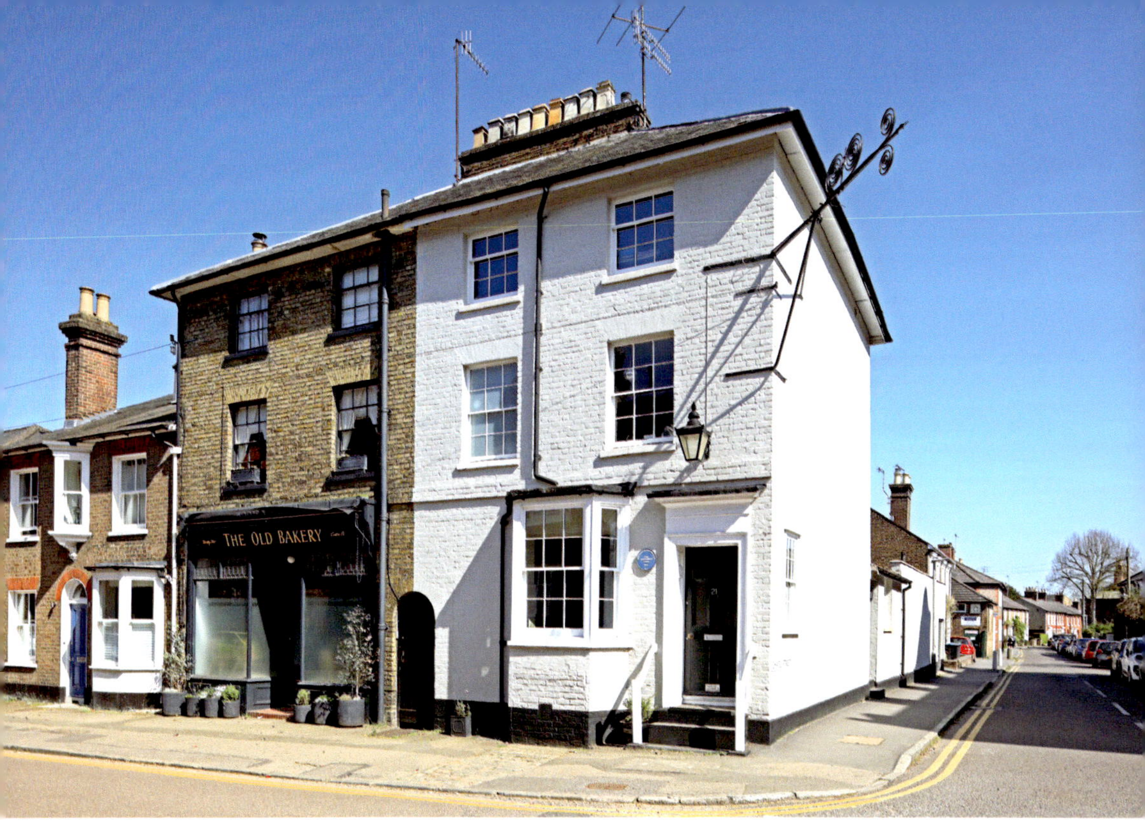

Another former public house, once the Gardener's Arms.

## 36. Admiral House

The *Bucks Herald* reported the death of Admiral George Cornish Gambier in June 1879. He was a well-known Berkhamsted resident and died '…at his residence in the High-street, in his 84th year. The gallant admiral was of a genial and benevolent disposition, always ready to assist in any good cause, and it is to be feared that at times his good nature was imposed upon. It is not very long since he responded to a toast of the Navy, at a dinner at the Kings Arms, but of late he has been confined to his room. The deceased admiral was deservedly respected, and will be much missed in the town'.

George was born in 1795 in Shenley, Hertfordshire. Even by the standards of the day, the Gambier family was large. He was one of fifteen children born to Samuel and Jane. On 18 June 1808, during the Napoleonic Wars, George, then twelve years old, entered the navy as a midshipman. He quickly rose through the ranks, visiting China, New South Wales, New Zealand, the western coast of South America, the Marquesas Islands, and Otaheite.

In 1821, he was posted to HMS *Dauntless* and made post captain. Promotion to post captain did not however guarantee continuing command of a ship, and that was George's fate. When HMS *Dauntless* returned from the Pacific in 1823,

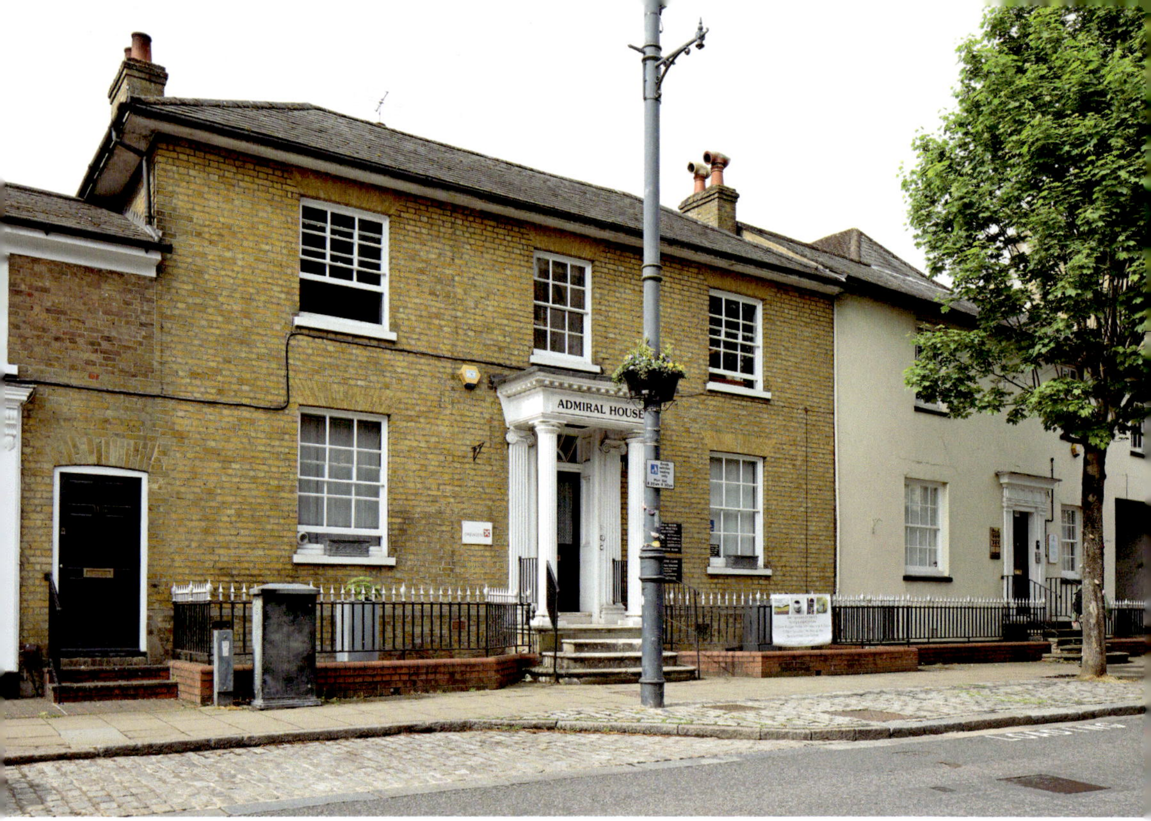

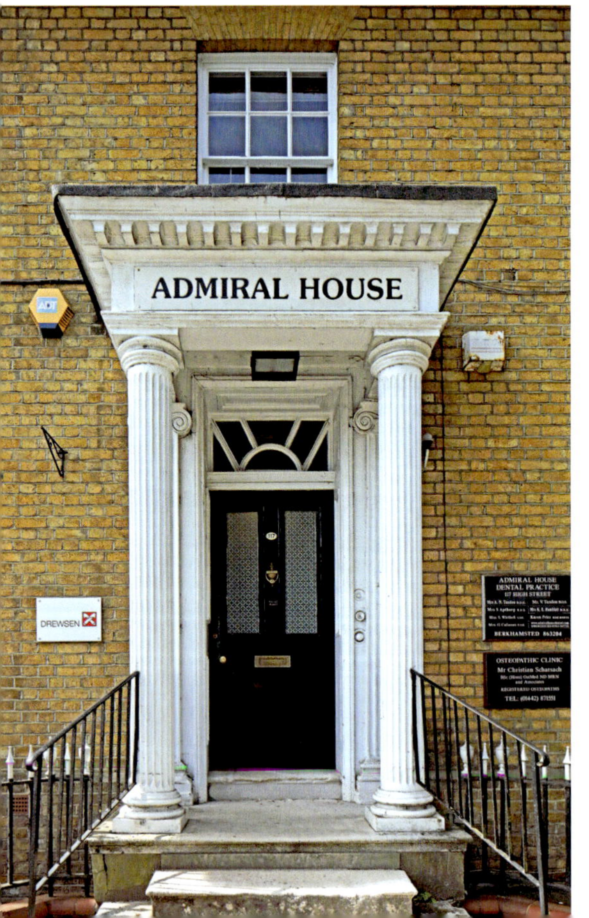

*Above*: Admiral House.

*Left*: A fine entrance to a house that was once the home of a very fine resident.

the ship was paid off and George, without a command, was 'on the beach' and reduced to half pay.

Despite his employment predicament, provided he did not die or disgrace himself, he was guaranteed to reach the rank of admiral. In 1852, George was promoted to the rank of retired rear admiral. In 1858, he became a retired vice admiral, and in 1863 he made the rank of retired admiral, all without having actually been to sea since 1823.

Although he may not have commanded a ship since 1823, George was actively involved with the welfare of sailors ashore, contributing substantial sums of his own money to providing for destitute sailors.

George became a confirmed bachelor and he never married. He seems to have spent his life ashore, staying with various members of his family and friends.

By 1871 George had moved to Berkhamsted and was living with his sister, Henrietta, on Berkhamsted's High Street. The house stands on the High Street opposite the junction with Castle Street and is today aptly named 'Admiral House'.

It was fairly common at this time for fights to break out between parties of boys from the town and boys from Berkhamsted School, not only with fists but also with snowballs often containing stones. Such fights, sometimes quite serious affairs, were enjoyed by George, who cheered them on.

## 31. Berkhamsted Railway Station

The construction of the railway through rural Hertfordshire was highly unpopular in the 1830s. Not only did it threaten the business interests of stagecoaches and coaching inns, but the landed gentry were strongly opposed to railway companies driving the 'iron horse' across their country estates.

Despite local opposition, the plans received royal assent, with the landowners succeeding in having the route of the railway diverted to avoid Gadebridge House and Ashridge. The railway line was built parallel to the Grand Junction Canal and the ruined barbican and moat of Berkhamsted Castle were cleared to make way for the embankment.

During the construction works, Berkhamsted experienced significant upheaval due to an influx of immigrant workers from the Midlands, northern England, Scotland and Ireland. Navvies filled the local pubs and drunken fights broke out nightly on the once-quiet Berkhamsted High Street, causing even further local resentment.

The building we see today is in fact the second railway station in Berkhamsted. The original opened in 1837 and was located 100 metres further along Lower Kings Road, closer to the Castle Street Bridge. It was replaced with the present building in 1875, when the railway was widened.

Occasionally, an individual connected to a building may be more interesting than the building itself. In this instance, George Blincow (1858–1928) served as stationmaster here for eighteen years – from 1903 until his retirement in 1921.

Blincow witnessed the change of Berkhamsted from a small, semi-rural town into a London commuter town, driven by the railways.

In those days, Lord Brownlow (Adelbert Brownlow-Cust, 3rd Earl Brownlow) had a special privilege at Berkhamsted station: his own private entrance and waiting room. As well as welcoming Lord and Lady Brownlow to the station, Blincow would also have met a number of noted people in high society and government who passed through the station en route to Ashridge.

In 1914–19, the fields to the north of Berkhamsted Castle were turned into an enormous campsite for the Inns of Court Officer Training Corps (OTC). Young men camped here trained for war, practising the techniques of trench warfare and artillery before heading off to fight in the battlefields of the First World War. Thousands of young men who were sent off to war passed through Berkhamsted station, where they were put on special trains bound for Southampton docks. There, they would be shipped over to the battlefields of France. Many others would be sent to Ireland, where they were engaged in the attempt to quell the Easter Rising. The man in charge of this complex and challenging operation was the stationmaster, George Blincow. He had to manage a nightly influx of thousands of troops from the Berkhamsted camp, St Albans, Luton, and elsewhere. Even the cavalry horses had to be coaxed onto the platforms and into goods wagons to be transported to the ports. Lord Brownlow gave up his private waiting room to be used as the Quartermaster's office and stores.

Of the Inns of Court OTC, 12,000 trainee officers passed through Berkhamsted; by the end of the First World War, over half were wounded and 2,200 had been killed in action. Among these trainee officers was George's own son, Archibald. He went to fight and was one of the lucky ones who survived the conflict and returned home. George Blincow retired in 1921 and died in 1928 at North Wembley. He lies buried in the upper section of Rectory Lane Cemetery.

After the Second World War had taken its toll on the nation, the railway companies were nationalised and merged into one body, British Railways, in 1948.

A very early view of the railway station.

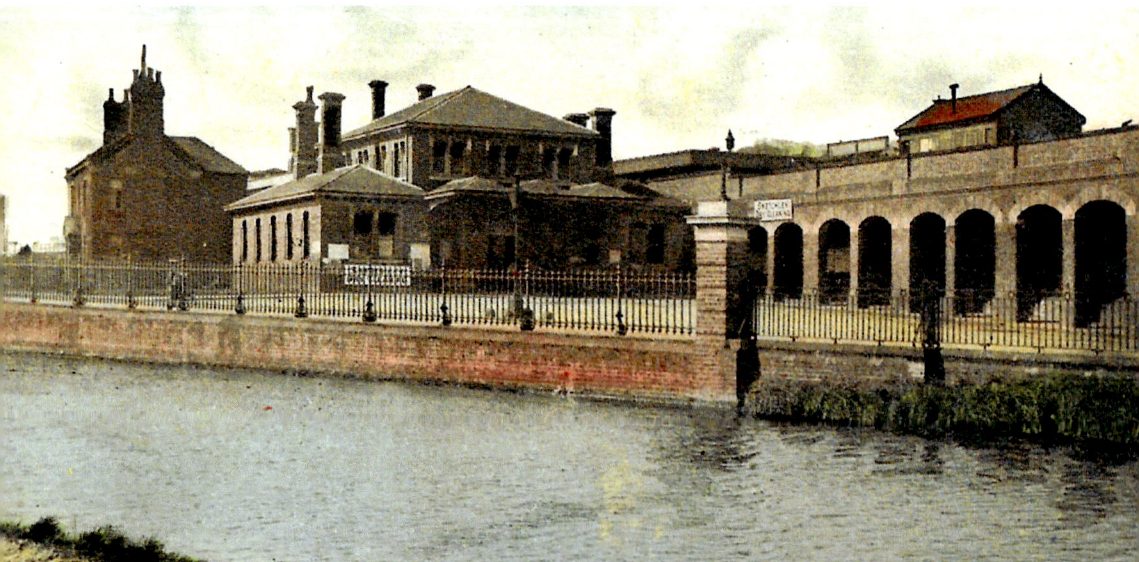

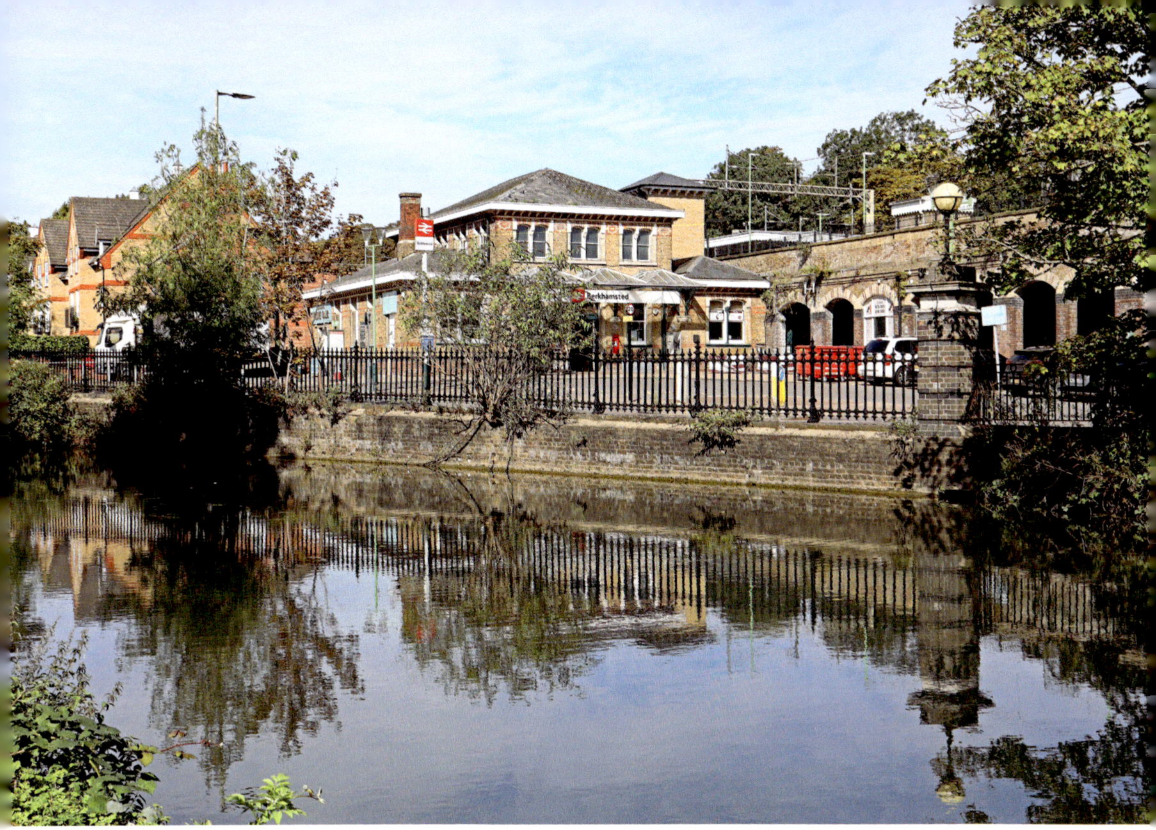

*Above*: The railway station today, a popular commuter connection into London.

*Below*: The second iteration of the town's railway station.

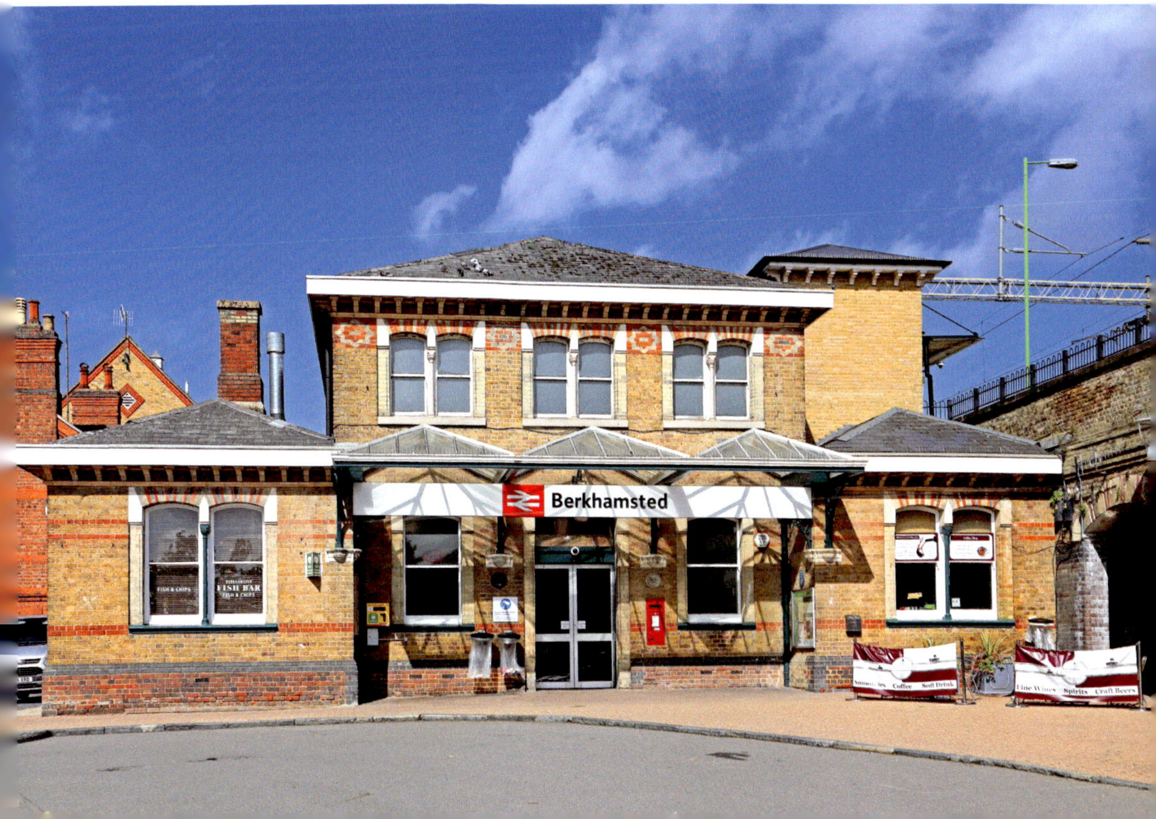

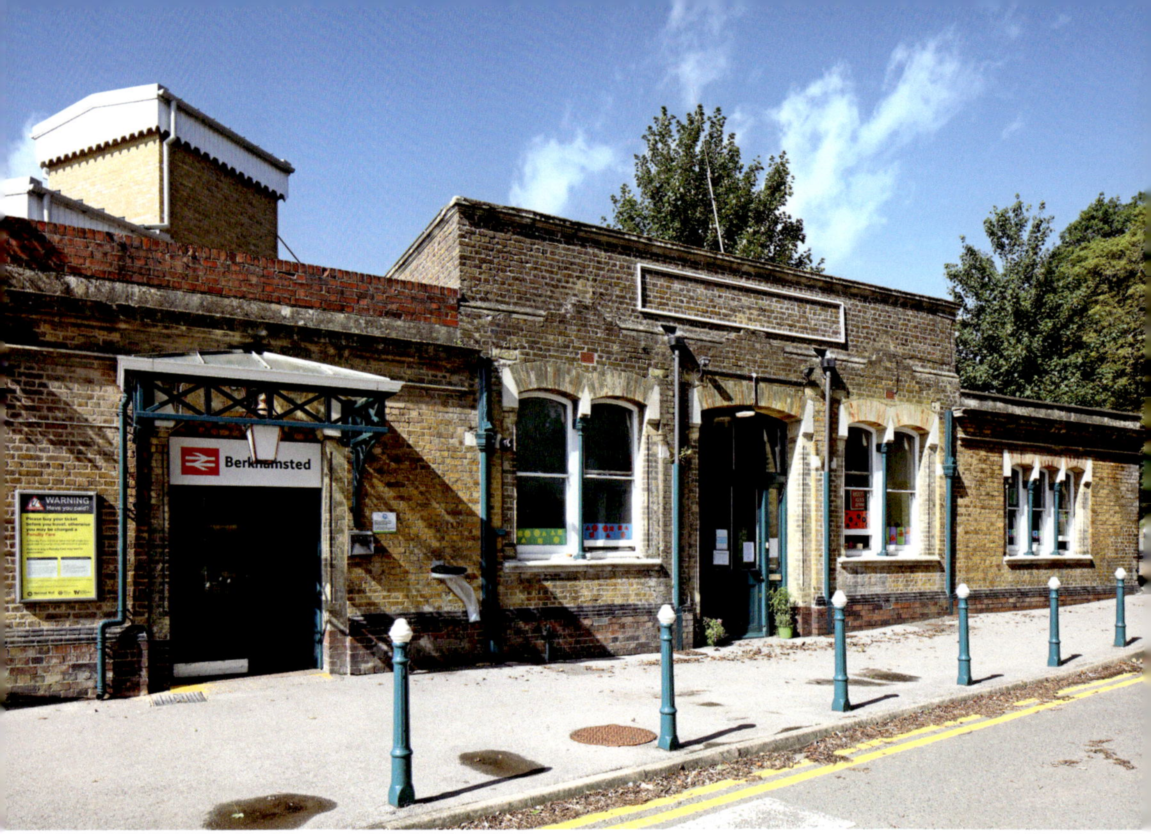

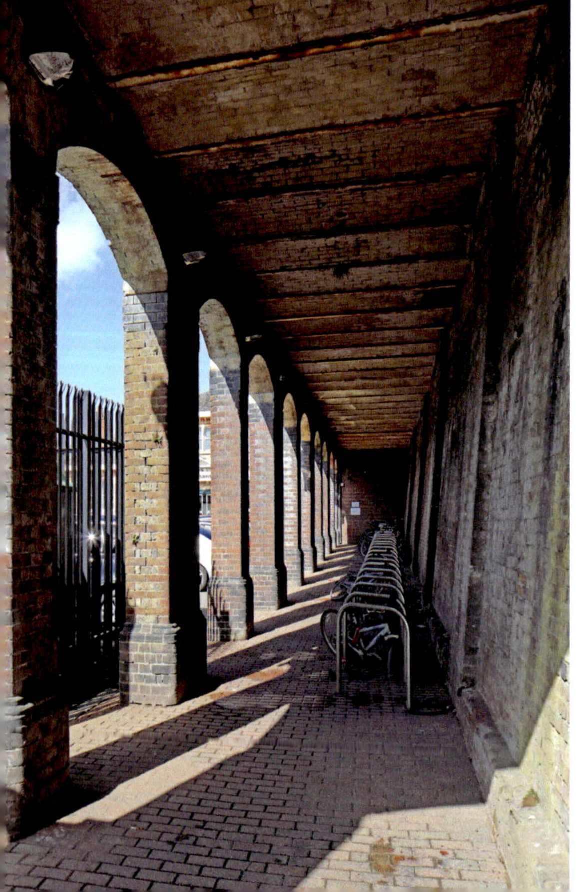

*Above*: Built in 1875, it has witnessed many local soldiers heading off to war.

*Left*: An architectural delight to this day, despite the incongruous railings.

Berkhamsted station continued under British Rail operation until the privatisation of the railways in the 1990s. Since then, Berkhamsted station has been served by an ever-changing succession of railway operators.

## 32. Kings Road Churches

There are two ecclesiastical buildings on Kings Road: one still in use and one no longer active. The Hope Hall was originally built in 1875 as a worship hall for the Plymouth Brethren by Samuel Alexander. In the 1860s, members of this Nonconformist, evangelical Christian denomination met in private houses for worship. They began a house church in a cottage in Castle Street, and as their numbers grew they began to use Prospect Place Wesleyan Chapel on Highfield Road, and their larger meetings took place in Berkhamsted Town Hall.

Samuel Alexander led the Brethren congregation from 1870. He was an inspirational preacher, and under his leadership they built their own meeting hall on Kings Road, the Hope Hall. In 1969 the Hope Hall was sold and continued as a place of Christian worship under the new name of the Kings Road Evangelical Church, remaining in use to this day.

Further along Kings Road is the rather quaint former Beulah Chapel. It was built in 1889 by the Strict Baptists, adjoining a row of four houses of the same period. There used to be an alley which led to a small garden at the rear. It was used for a period by the Girl Guides but was deemed too small for that use. Kelly's Directory of 1902 quoted it as being able to hold 120 sittings. Today it is residential.

Kings Road Church.

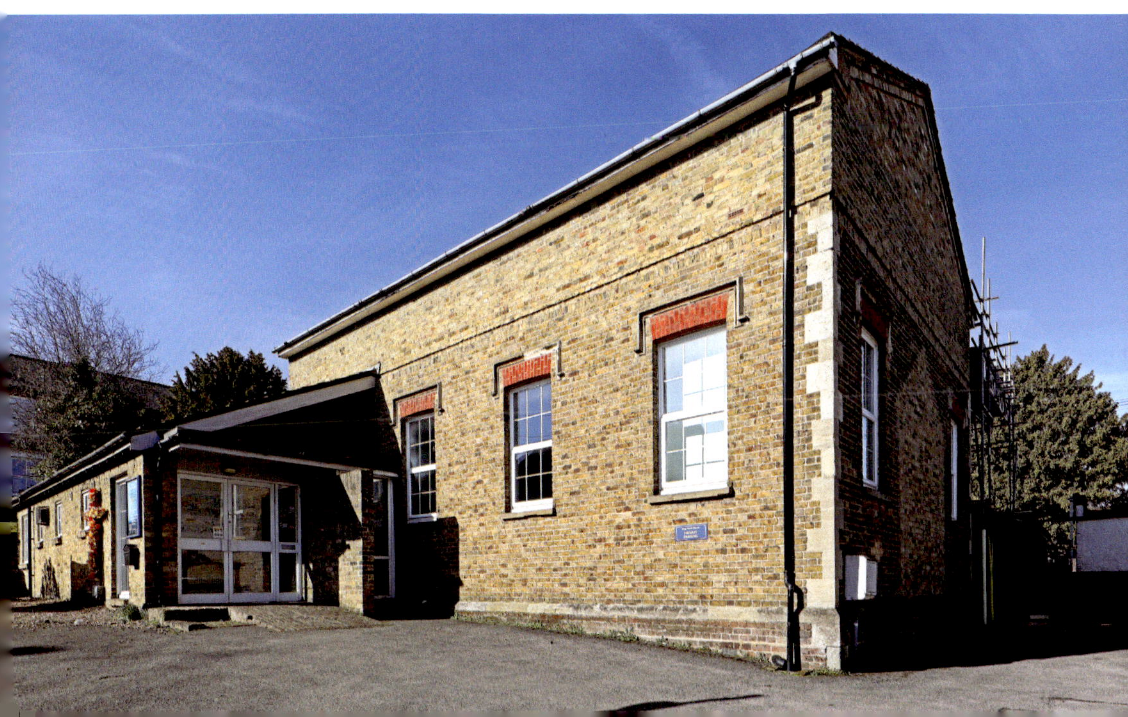

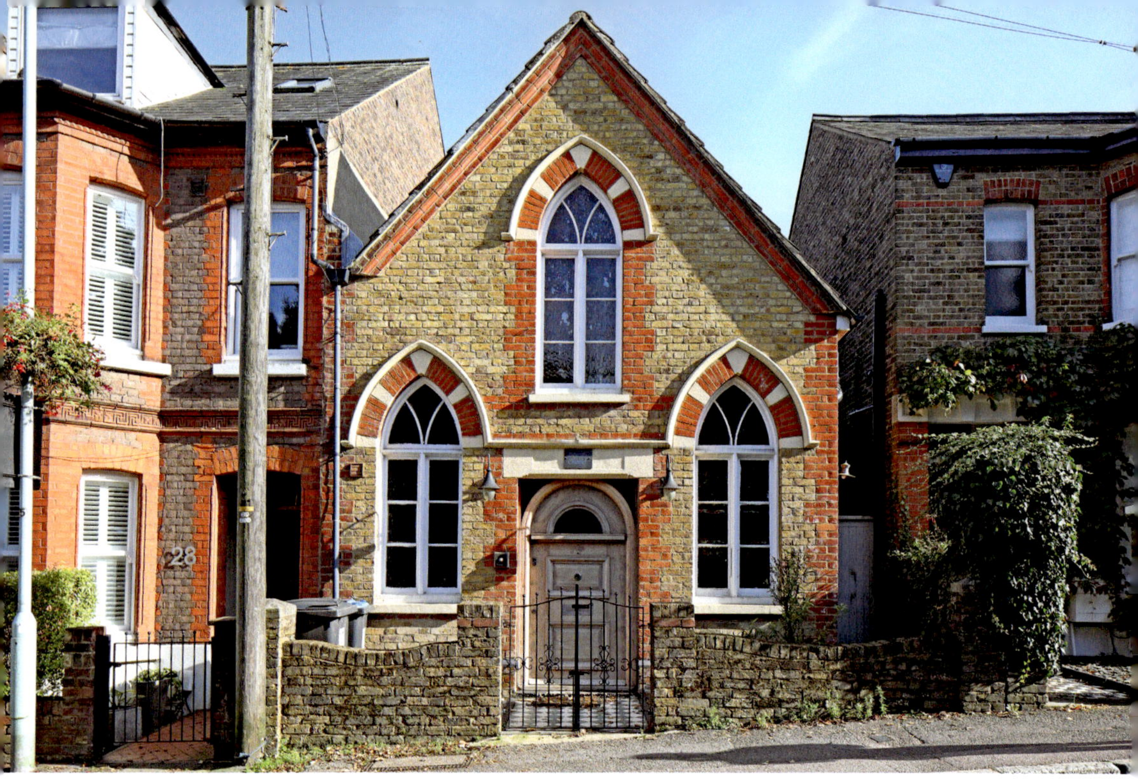

Former Beulah Chapel.

## 33. A. C. Meeks Livery and Hunting Stables

The brick building that stands on Lower Kings Road opposite the entrance to Waitrose car park is very unusual with a distinctive circular opening in the front gable. These premises were originally A. C. Meek's Livery and Hunting Stables, where horses would be kept for the owner, fed and cared for at a fixed charge. The circular opening was possibly the hatch to a hayloft.

Evidence survives today of the building's original purpose. On the north side of the building overlooking the River Bulbourne, an advertisement painted on the brickwork is still visible from the road.

Along with the stabling horses, the business also offered horse-drawn carriages for hire.

It is not known exactly when the building was erected, although Lower Kings Road was first laid out in 1885. The proprietor, Arthur Cecil Meek, appears in Kelly's Directory for 1899 as a jobmaster – a livery-stable keeper who also 'jobs out' horses and carriages. Telephones reached Berkhamsted in the 1890s, and so the inclusion of a telephone number suggests the sign was painted about 1900.

Meek's business did very well for a time and he employed a sizeable staff of coachmen and groomsmen. Unfortunately for Meek, advances in twentieth-century technology brought about great change with the advent of the motor car. Demand for horse-drawn transport reduced drastically, and Meek's business failed to adapt and closed sometime after 1915. Meek emigrated to Australia and died in Sydney in 1945.

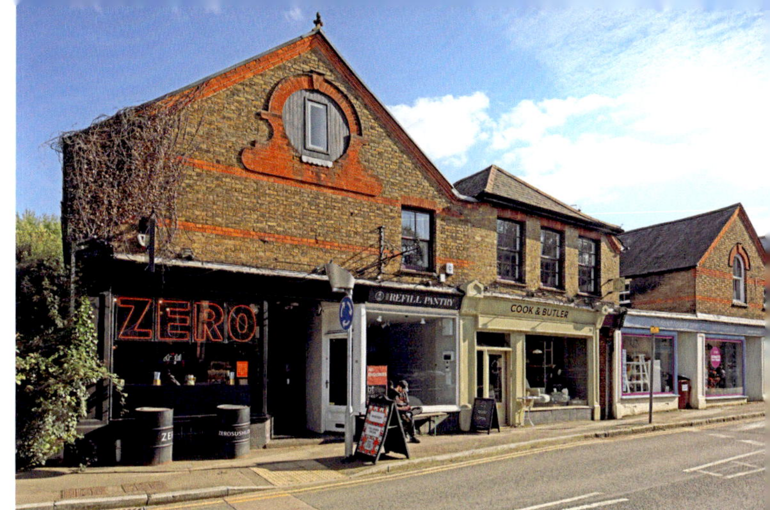

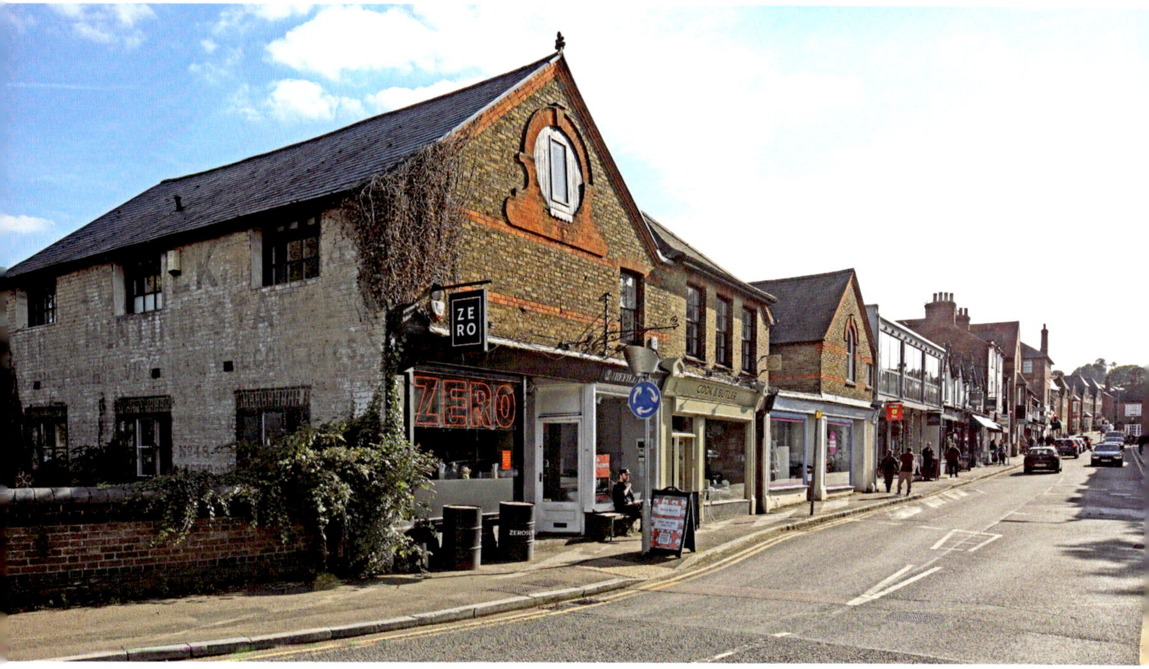

Sometime in the early twentieth century the livery stable was converted into a retail building and shopfronts were built, filling in the old stable yard. These shop units have had numerous tenants over the years.

## 34. Overton House

A house on the corner of Grubbs Lane (now Chesham Road), was purchased in 1888 by the headmaster, T. C. Fry. Known as Overton, the junior boarding house and its pupils were under the care of Mr G. H. Gowring. Both Overton and St John's were amongst the first houses to be lit by electricity in Berkhamsted, after Mr Gowring had installed a gas engine.

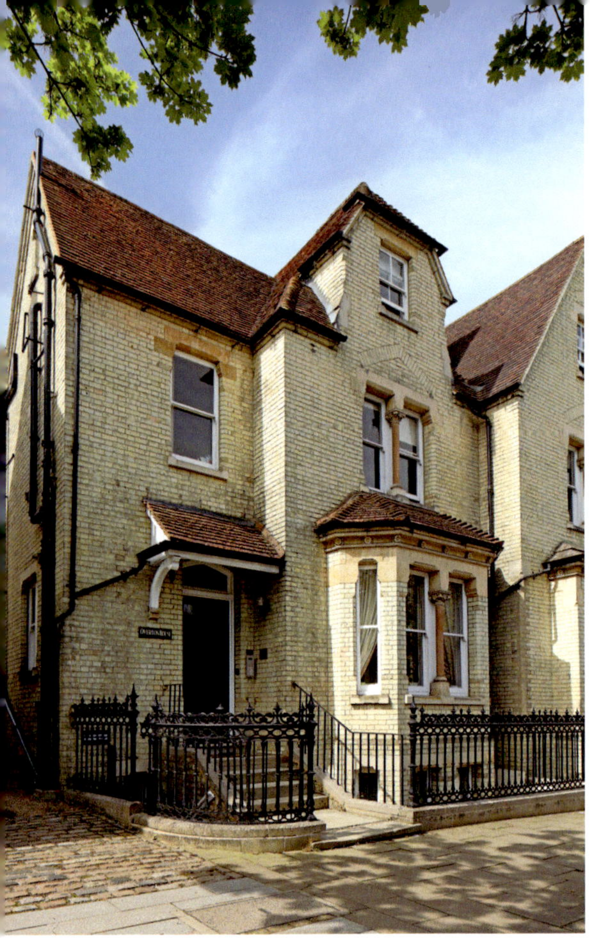

Overton House.

## 35. Clementine Churchill's Home, No. 107 High Street

In 1900, the young Clementine Hozier was brought to live Berkhamsted by her parents so that she could complete her education at Berkhamsted School for Girls. She lived at No. 107 High Street, overlooking the cemetery. This bright, young fifteen year old was the daughter of Lady Blanche Hozier and moved in high social circles. In her teens she fell in love with the painter Walter Sickert and the MP Sir Sidney Peel. Her affairs of the heart after leaving Berkhamsted eventually led her into a romance with a young politician named Winston Churchill. They married in 1908, a marriage that established Clementine's notability as the wife of the celebrated wartime prime minister.

During the Second World War, Clementine was chairman of the Red Cross Aid to Russia Fund, the president of the YWCA War Time Appeal. In 1946, she was appointed a Dame Grand Cross of the Order of the British Empire. After Winston's death in 1965, she was created a life peer as Baroness Spencer-Churchill and sat in the House of Lords. She died in 1977 and is buried at St Martin's Church, Bladon, Oxfordshire. In 1979 her youngest daughter, Baroness Soames, unveiled a plaque on Clementine's Berkhamsted house.

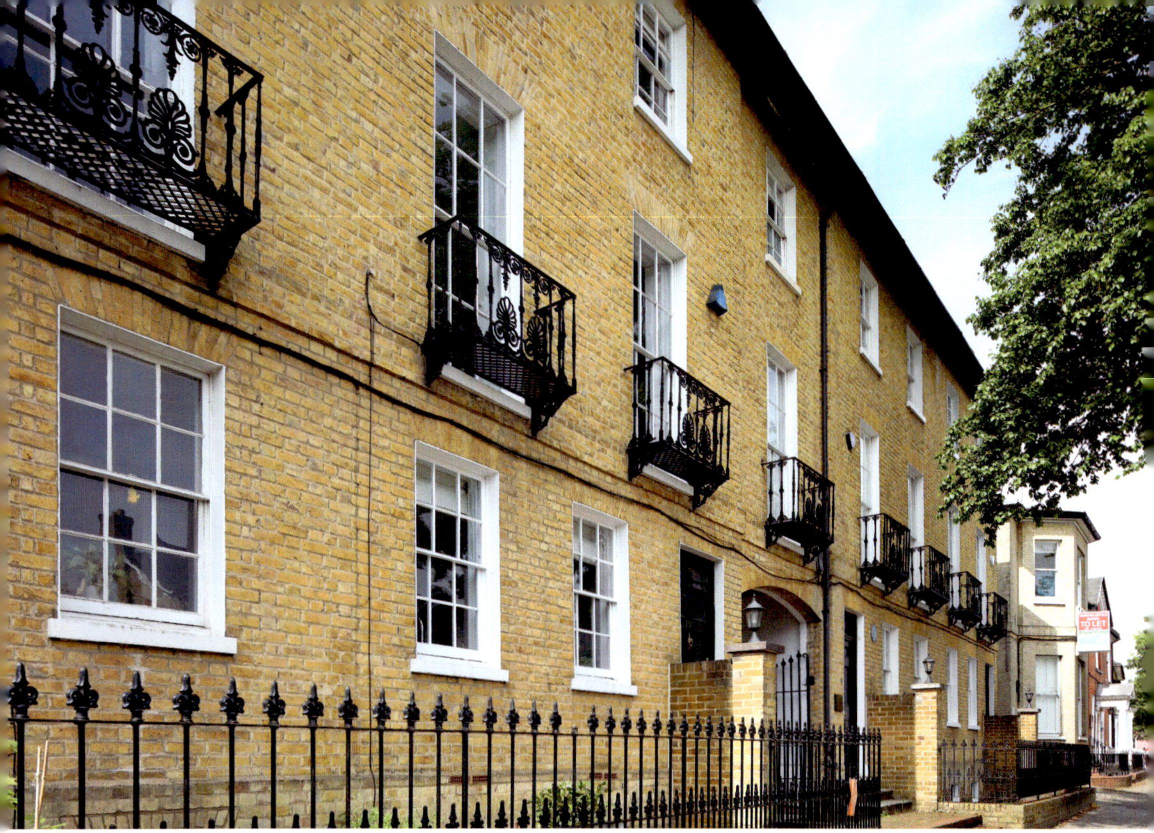

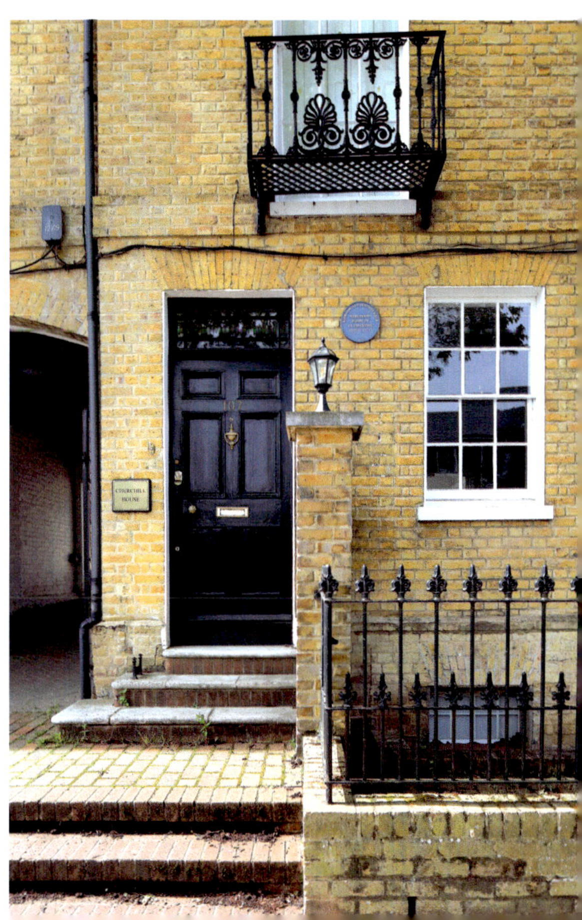

*Above*: The former home of Clementine Churchill.

*Right*: A grand entrance for a once very formidable resident.

## 36. Graham Greene's Birthplace

Henry Graham Greene was born in Berkhamsted in 1904, the fourth of six children of Charles Henry Greene, a schoolteacher, and his wife Marion. He was educated at Berkhamsted School, where his father was headmaster, but was bullied so relentlessly while a boarder that he tried to kill himself. Aged sixteen years old, he ran away from school and was sent by his parents to London for psychiatric treatment, spending six months under the care of a psychoanalyst. Greene returned to complete his schooling as a day boy, and it was at this point that he began writing what he later called 'the most sentimental fantasies in bad poetic prose'.

Berkhamsted, with which he was associated and around, provided many settings which were created in several of his works, particularly *The Human Factor* and *The Captain and the Enemy* and the short stories 'The Innocent', and

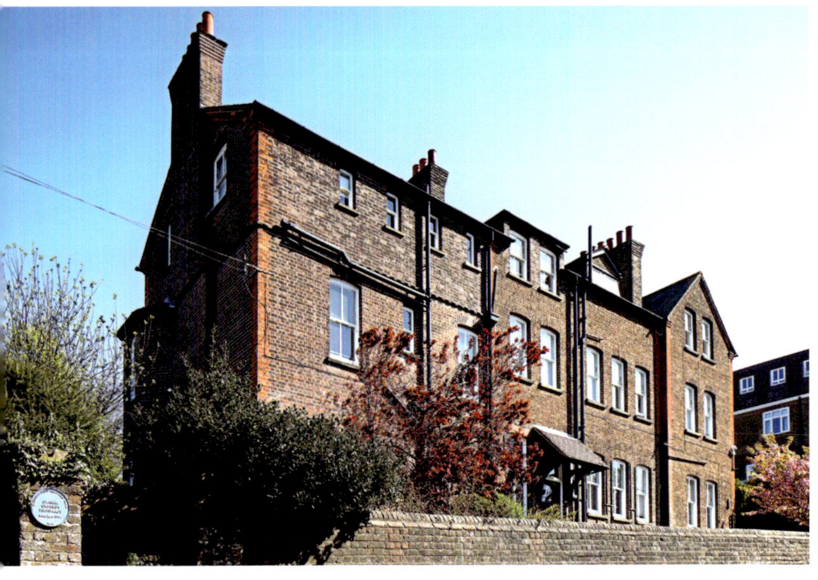

The birthplace of one of the town's most famous sons, author Graham Greene.

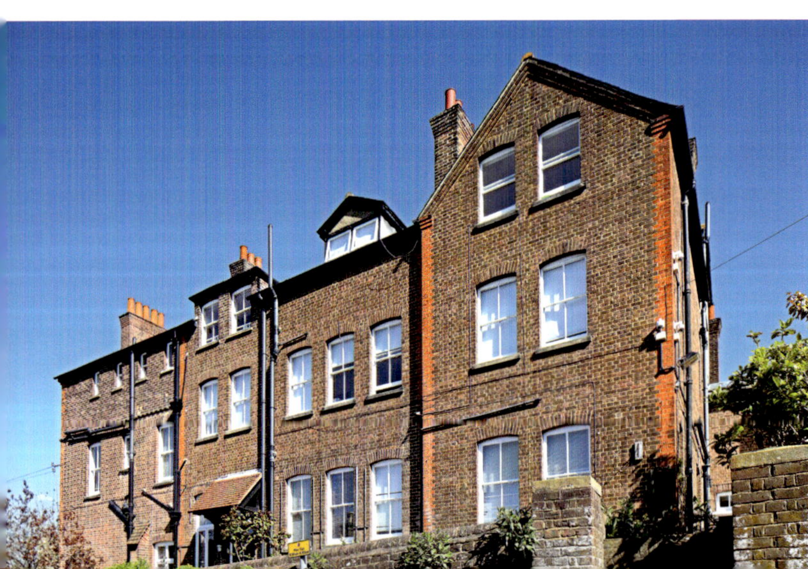

'Doctor Crombie' – although the town was sometimes given a different name. The influences of Graham Greene's early life in Berkhamsted, which moulded his character, his emotions and his memories, are reflected in much of his writing. His official biographer, Norman Sherry, referring to Graham Greene's personal map, says it is 'a map not simply of physical features but one on which were traced emotional and psychological contours mapping his development from childhood to adolescence and forming a personal historical addition to the history of the town'.


## 37. All Saints' Church

All Saints' Church is an early twentieth-century red-brick building that stands on the corner of Cross Oak Road and Shrublands Road. The housing expansion in the Kitsbury area of the town in the late nineteenth century meant that there was a requirement for a new church to accommodate the growing population. Kitsbury worshippers were having to attend services in a barn in Kitsbury Road behind the Berkhamsted Union Workhouse (now the Kitsbury Parade shops), and later in a 'Tin Tabernacle' on Cross Oak Road, which was a temporary church made of corrugated iron.

Revd Arthur Johnson, the rector of St Peter's (1883–1902), and Lord Brownlow obtained permission to build a 'chapel-of-ease' to meet local religious needs and relieve the demand on St Peter's Parish Church located further down the High Street. The foundation stone of All Saints was laid in 1905. Many local volunteers assisted in the laying of the buildings foundations. The main body of building was erected by Mr F. Harrowell of Tring.

The church's architect was Charles Henry Rew, who along with his son Noel Ackroyd Rew worked on designs for the new church. Rew had previously designed Berkhamsted School Chapel on Castle Street. Rew's original plans included twin towers at an extended western end of the church, although these were never realised. A number of fittings were brought from St Peter's Parish Church to adorn the new Kitsbury Church and included a fragment of a Norman font that was built into the chancel wall as well as a marble font that was given to St Peter's in 1662.

In 1915, a three-manual pipe organ built by Kirkland of London was installed in All Saints', having been dismantled and brought from All Saints' Church in Tufnell Park, London.

All Saints', Berkhamsted, had a thriving congregation, but despite this, the church closed in 1923 due to lack of funds, though reopened again in 1938 after significant fundraising efforts. In the 1970s, All Saints merged with the Methodist Church to form an Anglican/Methodist Local Ecumenical Partnership. The Methodist Chapel on the High Street closed and was demolished and is now the site of a pizza restaurant.

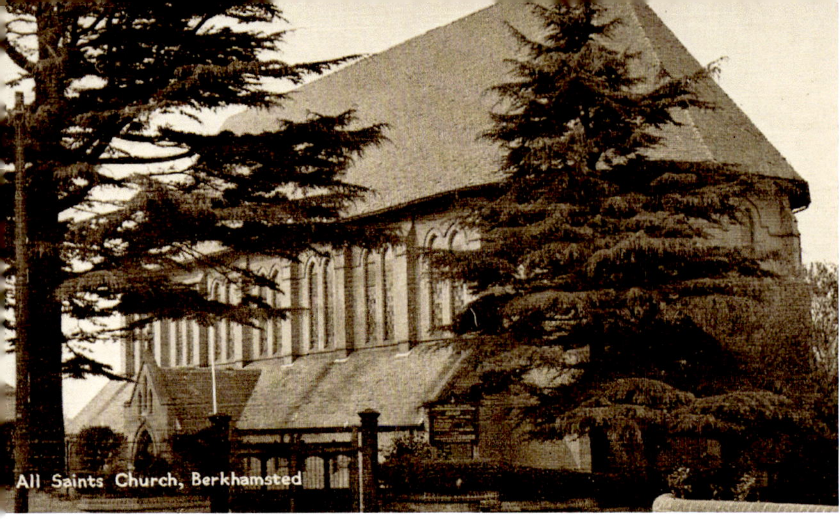


*Left*: An early view of All Saints' Church.

*Below*: The present-day All Saints' Church.

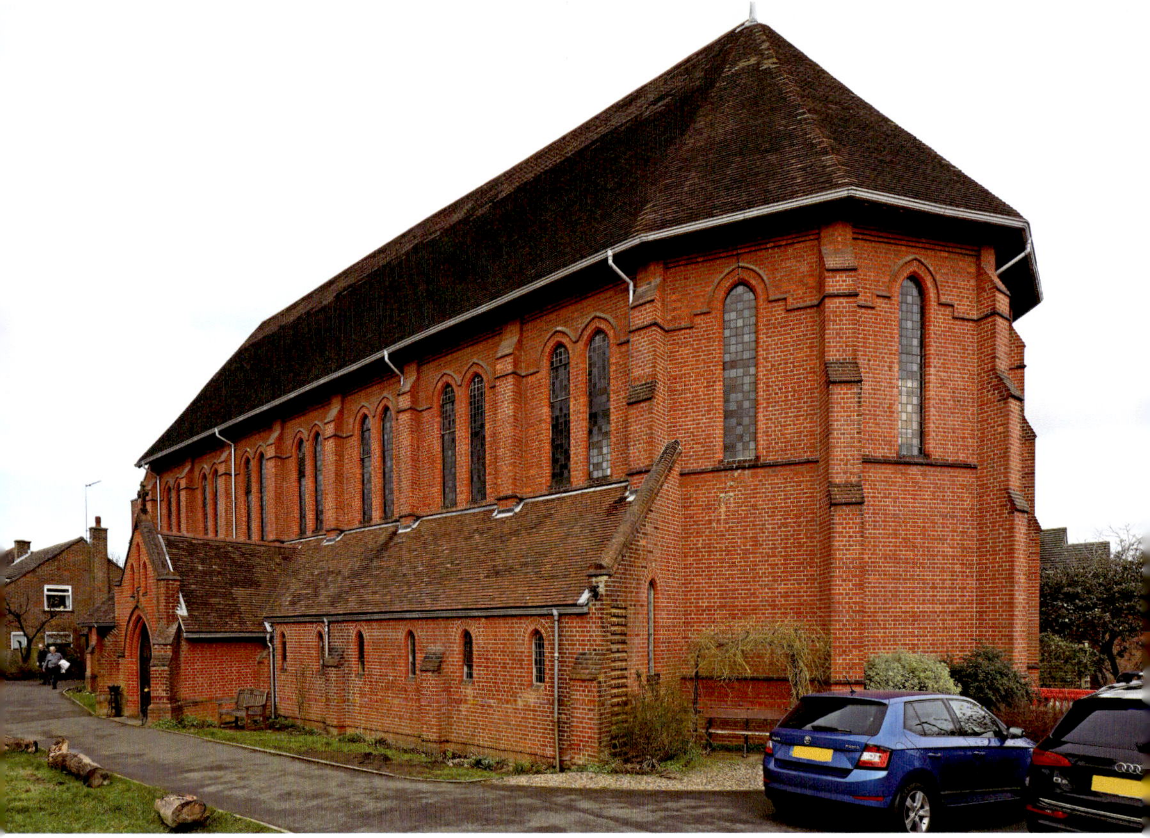

## 38. The Mansion

This house was designed by George Hubbard and built by H. & J. Matthews between 1906 and 1908 for Sir John Evans. Evans was a well-known archaeologist and geologist who became president of the Geological Society of London. Evans called the house Britwell, but after his death 1908 it was bought by Sir Arthur Cory Wright, a businessman, who renamed it Berkhamsted Hill.

The house was bought by the Deen family in 1919 and by Sir Richard Ashmole Cooper, a businessman, in 1937. After Cooper's death in 1946, the house was acquired by his family chemicals business, which itself was bought by the Wellcome Trust in 1959. The house next came into the ownership of the Pitman-Moore Company, a pharmaceuticals business, who had no further use for it after 1991. Now known as 'the Mansion', it became the centre point of a retirement facility known as 'Castle Village' in 1999.

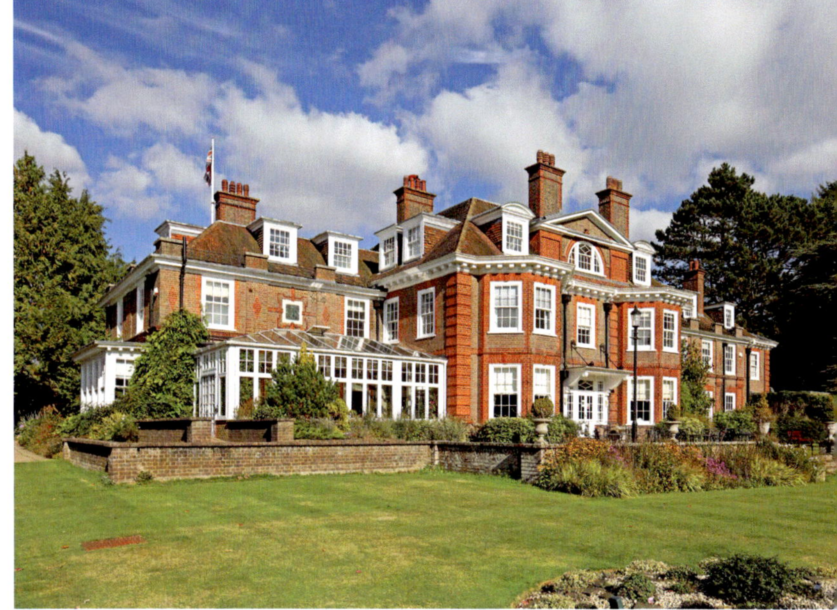

*Right*: The Mansion, once the home of a famous archaeologist and geologist.

*Below*: Castle Village retirement facility.

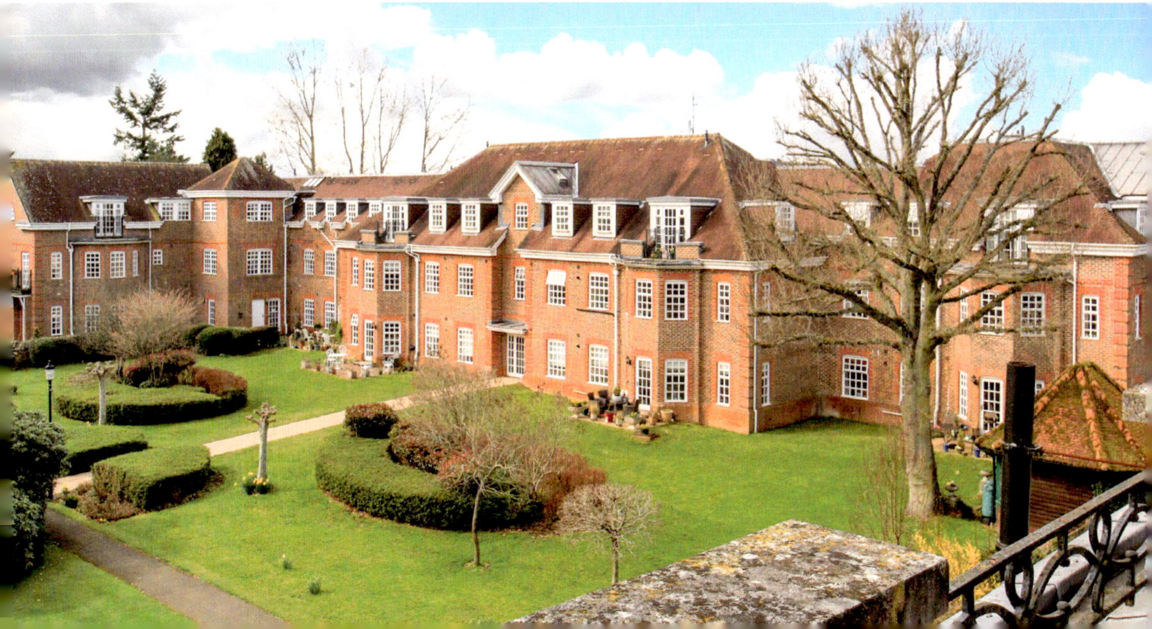

## 39. Sunnyside Church

The Church of St Michael and All Angels at Sunnyside is a picturesque, early twentieth-century church. Like All Saints' Church (1906) on the other side of the town, it was designed by the architect Philip M. Johnston FRIBA to meet the needs of a newly established congregation. From 1881, worshippers in the Sunnyside area of Berkhamsted met for services in a converted barn on George Street. As the congregation grew in numbers, new premises were needed. Adelbert Brownlow-Cust, 3rd Earl Brownlow, donated a tract of nearby land and parishioners built a temporary corrugated-iron church there – basically a 'tin tabernacle' – in 1886.

Rew & Son drew up plans for a replacement stone church in the style of a traditional Sussex parish church. Parishioners raised money and volunteers helped to lay the foundations. The church was to be clad in flint, and there happened to be a ready supply of materials left over from William Butterfields' 1887 renovation work on St Peter's Parish Church in the town centre.

Construction work went ahead with substantial financial support for the chancel from local industrialist Sir Richard Powell Cooper, one of the directors of Coopers chemical works (buried in Rectory Lane Cemetery). Sunnyside Church was consecrated on 30 June 1909.

Various additions were made to the fabric of the church, including a 1916 stained-glass window dedicated to Edward Mawley, president of the National Rose Society, who is buried in Rectory Lane Cemetery. A carved oak chair designed by C. H. Rew was also placed in the church in memory of Herbert Henry Cooper.

The old 'tin taberrnacle' remained in use for many years as a church hall until it was demolished in 1983 and the Cedars flats were built on the site.

Sunnyside Church.

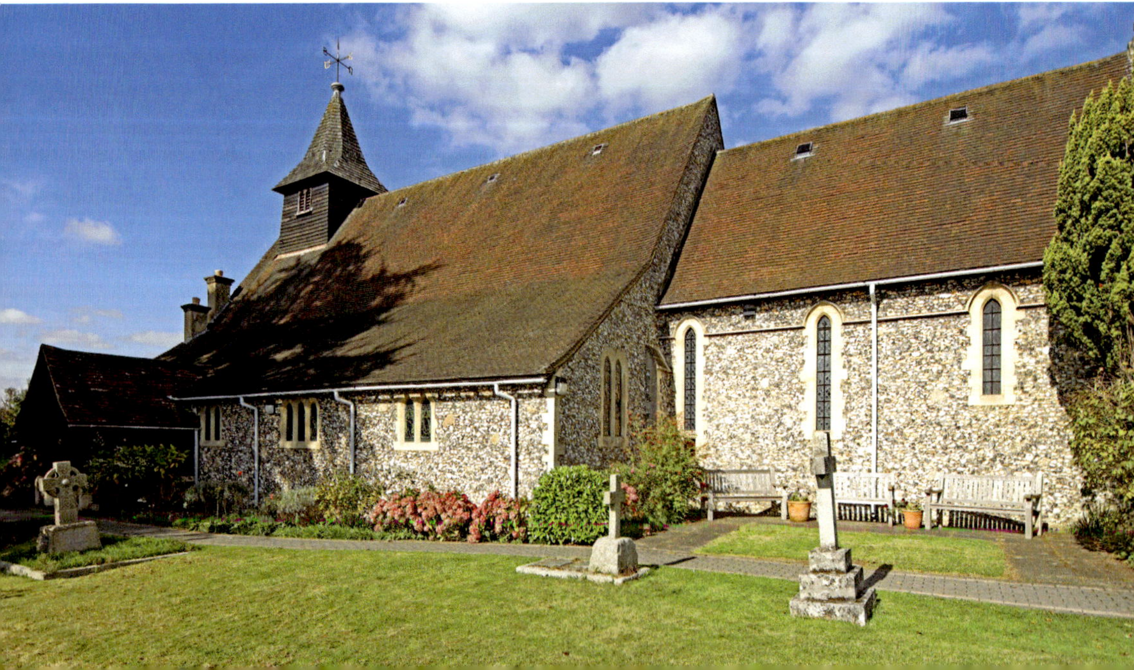

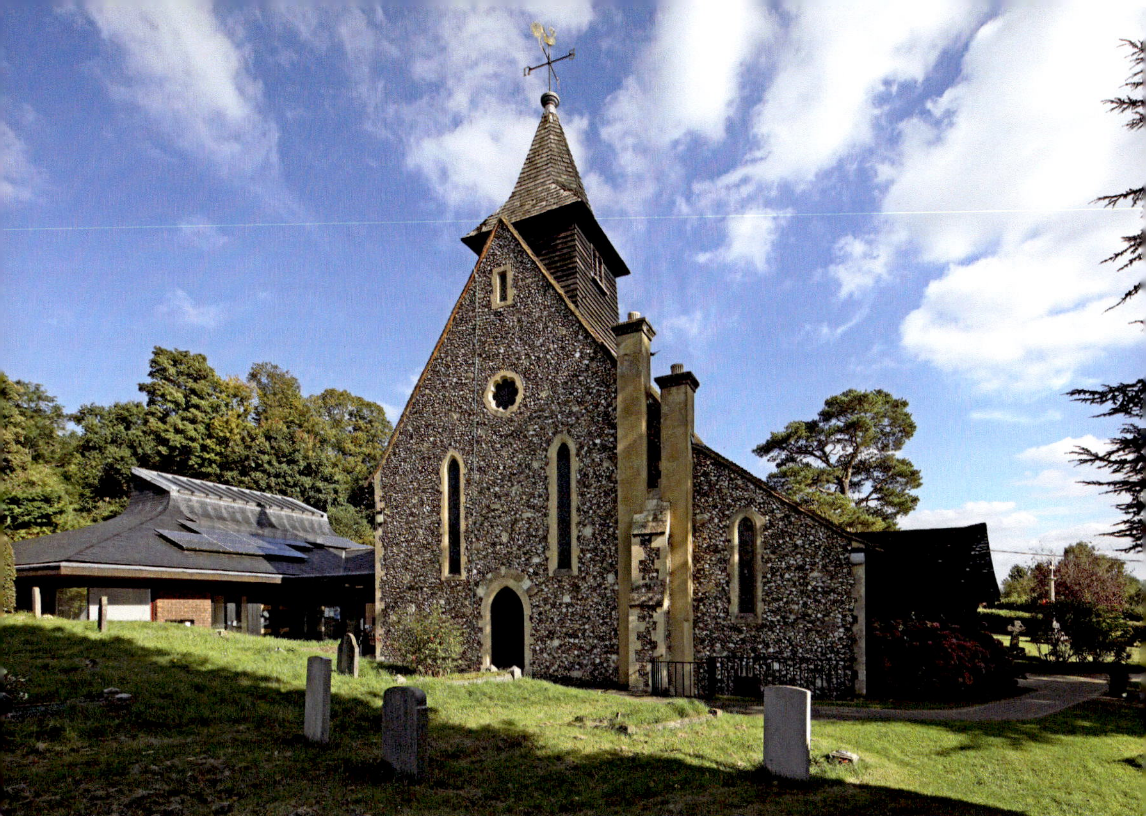

Sunnyside Church and its fantastic flint façade.

## 40. Castle Mill

The Domesday Book of 1086 refers to two mills in Berkhamsted with a combined value of 20s. One gave its name to Mill Street and was known as Castle Mill or simply Upper Mill in order to distinguish it from the Lower Mill or Bank Mill, sometimes referred to as Nether Mill, on Bank Mill Lane. The River Bulbourne provided the power to drive the waterwheels of both corn mills.

Upper Mill is referred to as Castle Mill in early documents not only because of its close proximity to the castle but also because it ground the flour, which would have been used in the castle kitchens.

The mill and a number of the mill cottages were demolished in 1926 when the music department buildings of Berkhamsted were developed. The mill stones can be seen in the school's gardens. A commemorative wall was built over the mill race in Mill Street with a Latin inscription which translates as: 'Here for a thousand years the old mills stood And gave us bread; Here now our School in the rival motherhood Feeds minds instead.'

Lower Mill was situated on Bank Mill on the site that is now occupied by the Old Mill House Hotel. An eighteenth-century lease refers to the fittings of the mill, which in the kitchen included a spit rack and a bacon rack in addition to two bars in the windows.

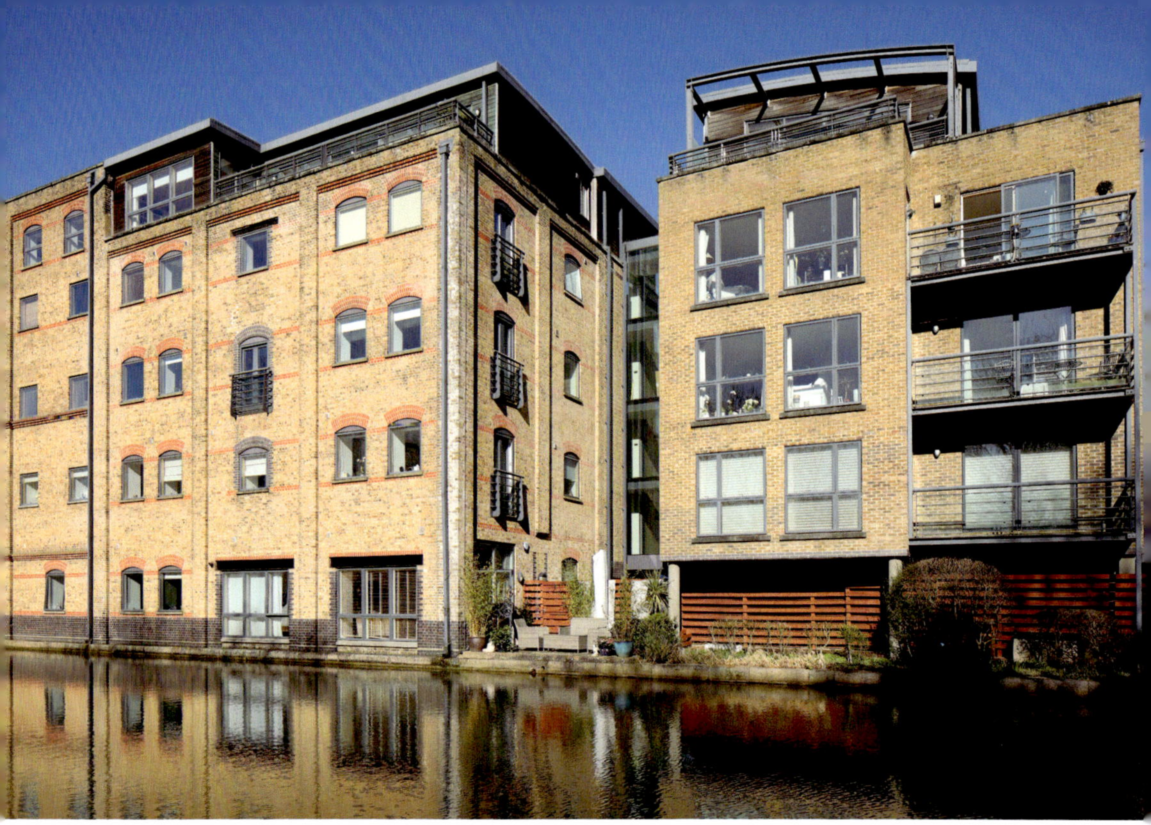

*Above*: Castle Mill, once industrial, now occupied by more sedate businesses.

*Below*: A canal setting for the once busy Castle Mill.

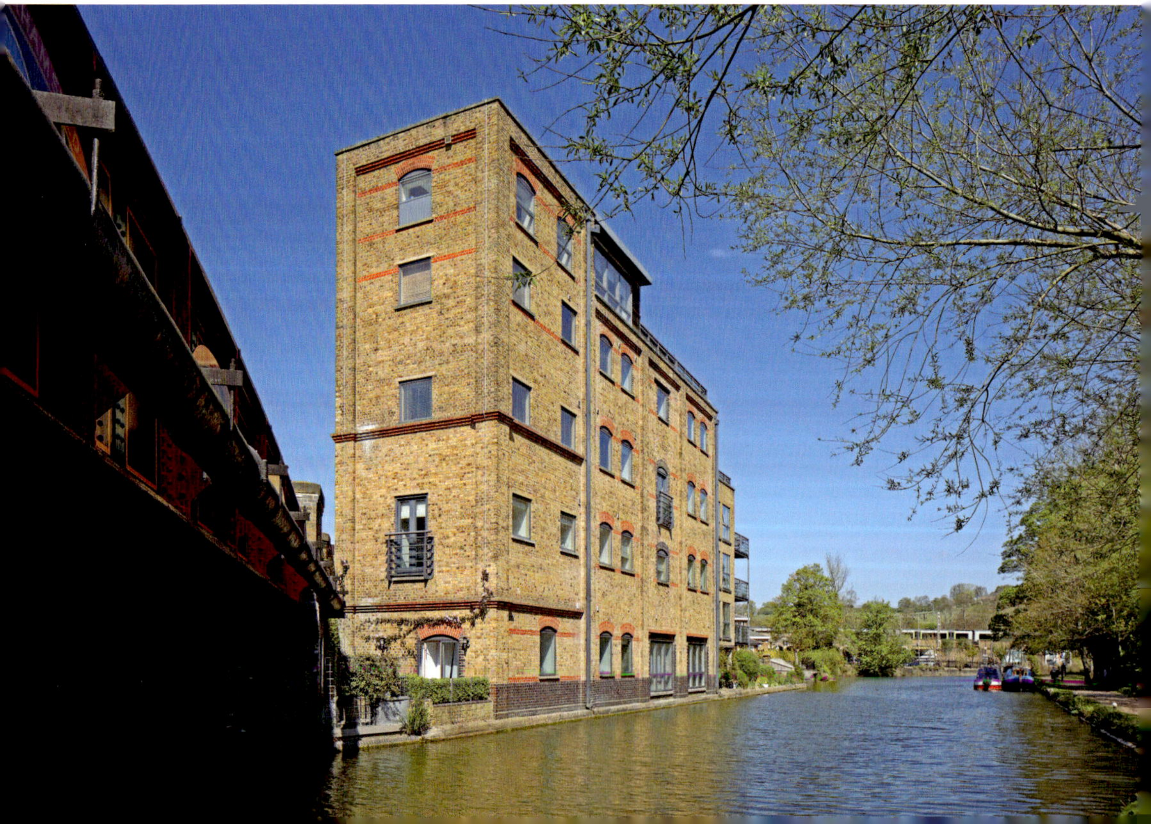

By the early 1900s the River Bulbourne had begun to dry up around Lower Mill. This lack of water, which was needed to drive the waterwheel, meant that the mill was forced to close. A serious fire in the 1890s caused a great deal of damage to the machinery and structure of the mill. The iron watermill remained in situ for many years until it was eventually removed for wartime salvage.

In 1910, Castle Mill or Knowles Mill was built by the bridge at Lower Kings Road. The mill was built for J. G. Knowles & Son, corn forage and seed merchants, and was used to manufacture animal feed. The mill took full advantage of its position, with a small wharf allowing grain to be delivered at one side of the building by canal boat, whilst wagons transported grain by road on the opposite side of the mill. It later became a subsidiary of Hovis Ltd. The mill closed after the Second World War and is now occupied by offices.

## 41. H. H. Dickman, Chemist

A Victorian house with chemists at ground floor, this late nineteenth-century house was converted to chemist use in 1914 with the shopfront and fittings dating from 1920. Dickman's are one of the longest-serving family businesses in Berkhamsted, dating as far back as the 1890s. The frontage is ornate and certainly worthy of its Grade II listed status, built of brick and with an ornate, glazed, wood frame shopfront. The ground floor is the shop with offices to the rear and residential and secondary shop accommodation at upper levels.

H. H. Dickman, chemist.

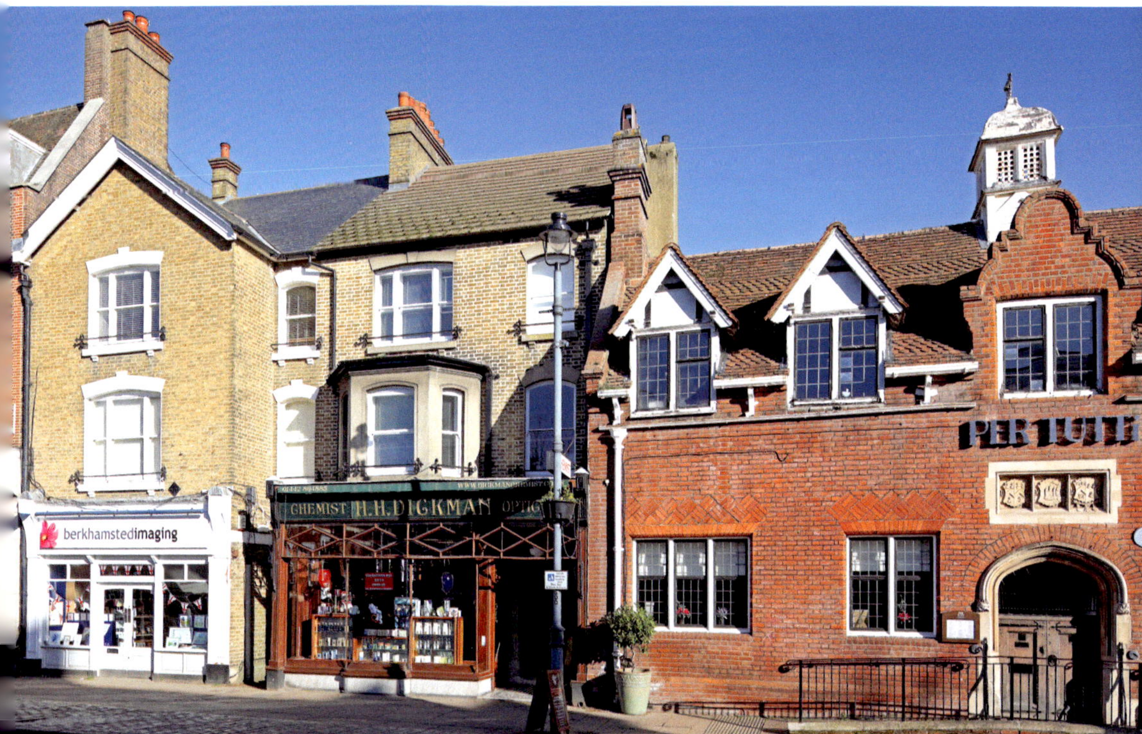

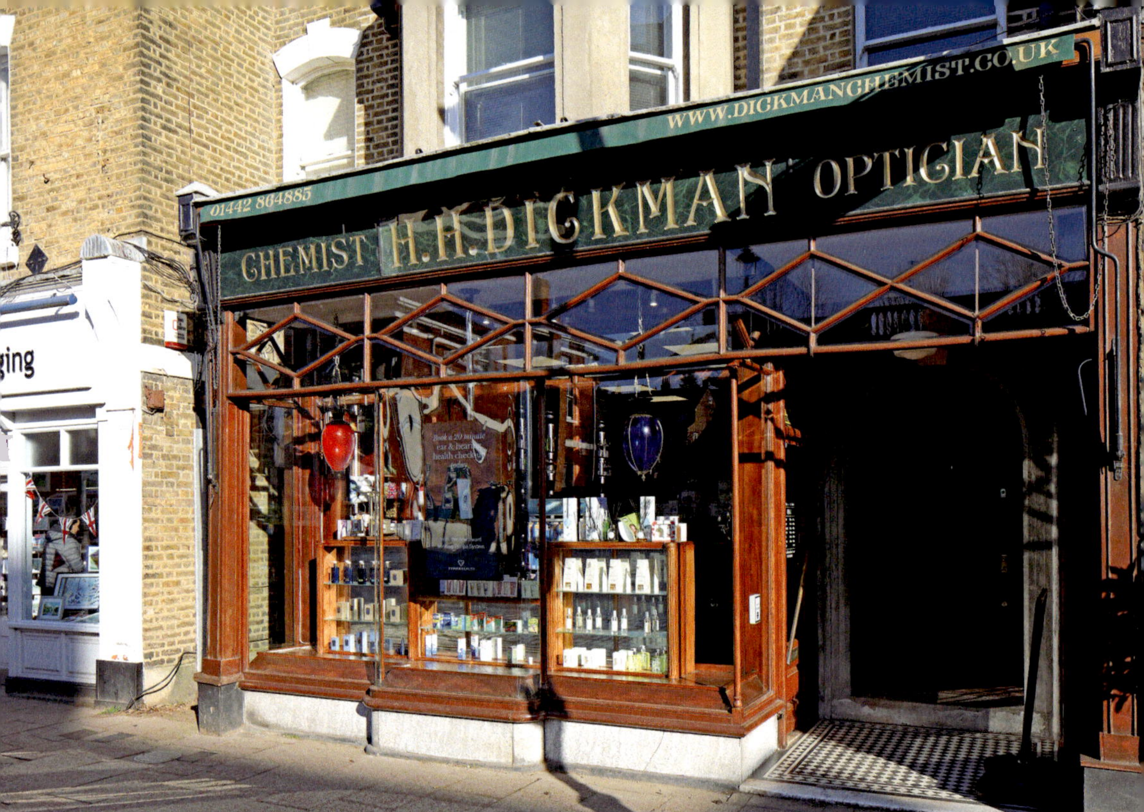

The chemist H. H. Dickman has been a long-serving family business in the town.

The property was also known as Linden House and the name can still be seen carved in the stone arch above the door. In the 1901 census both Hubert Henry Dickman and his older brother Charles were working as photo mechanical printers, but that line of work did not appeal to Hubert as in 1911 he had given up that occupation to become a pharmaceutical student. He was evidently successful in his studies and became a chemist.

## 42. The Beeches

The Beeches is a large house on Kings Road in the town. During the First World War it was used as a hospital by the Voluntary Aid Detachment (VAD), a voluntary unit of civilians who provided nursing care for military personnel. It was known as 'the Detention Hospital'. Nursing Sister Hannah Maude Cottingham was matron here during the war. Originally from Downpatrick in Northern Ireland, Sister Cottingham died of influenza in 1918 during the Spanish flu epidemic.

At the time, the Inns of Court OTC had a large army training camp in Berkhamsted. Affected by the death of a young woman who died far from home in the service of her country, the trainee officers paid for her memorial in Rectory Lane Cemetery.

The Beeches was later converted into a girls' school, becoming part of Berkhamsted School for Girls. In 1996, it became part of the Berkhamsted School.

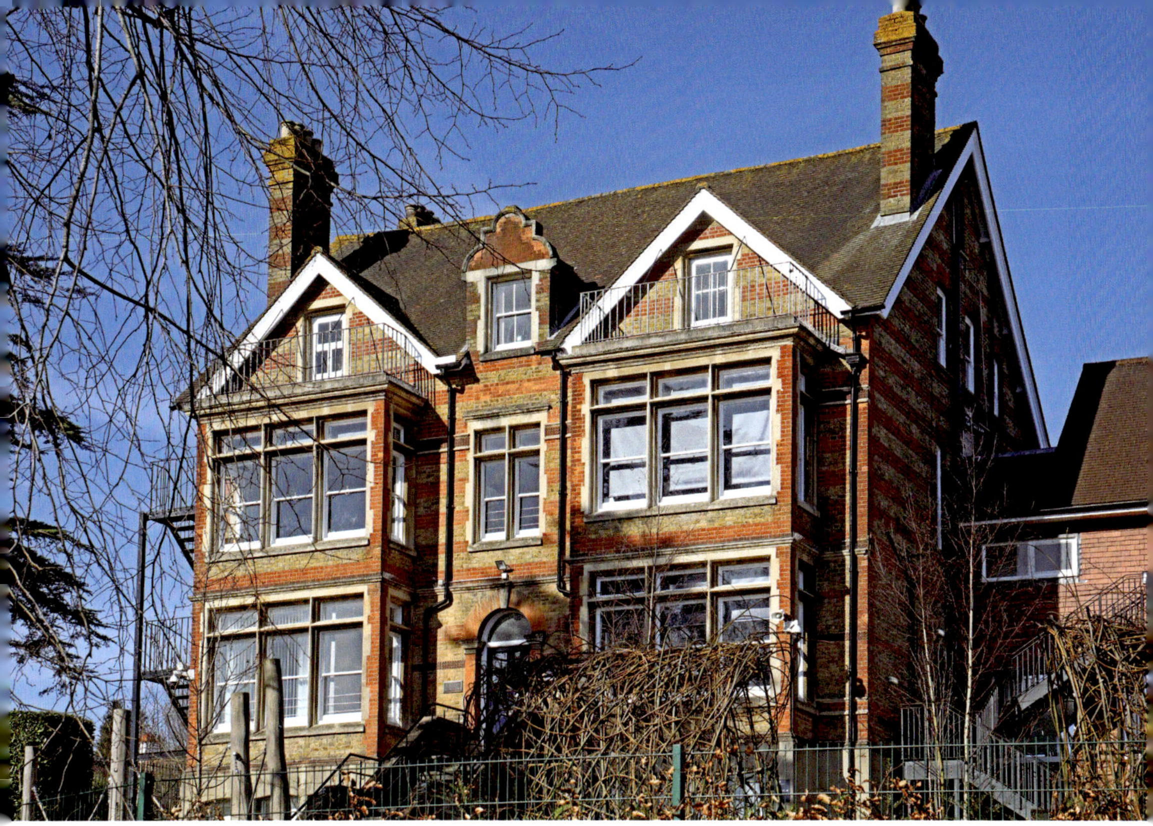

The Beeches, now part of a busy school but once used as a hospital.

## 13. No. 90 High Street

Berkhamsted & District Co-operative Society were present in Berkhamsted and had several small shops in multiple locations across the town, including here at No. 90 High Street and on the corner of Manor Street. These businesses prospered and were often in fine and rather elegant buildings. The building today is now a chemist.

The name of Hubert Figg lives on in this prominent town centre business.

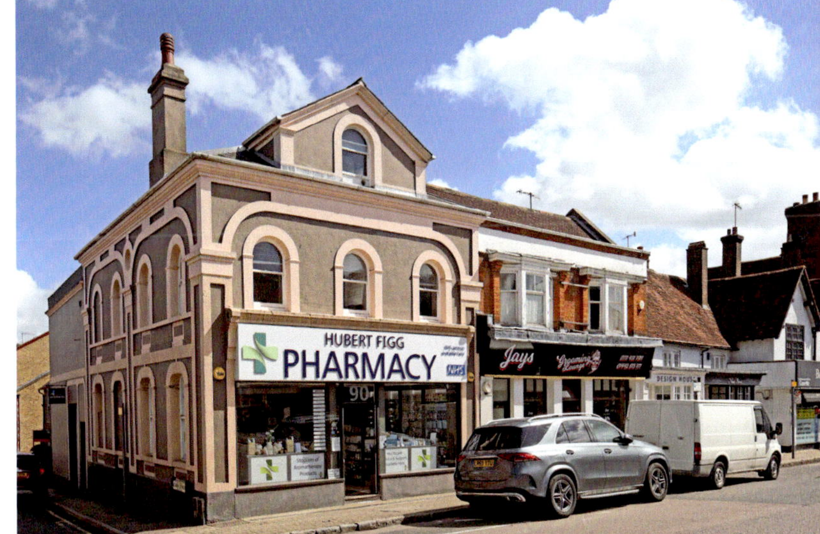

Hubert Figg was a well-known 'chemist and druggist' operating in Berkhamsted from July 1912. At that time, he was registered at No. 262 High Street but moved to No. 145 High Street in 1921, although this is confusing today as the High Street was renumbered in 1950 and the building became No. 173. He remained here until he ceased being the proprietor of the pharmacy during 1965. The name now lives on here in this pharmacy in this former Co-op building.


## 44. Home and Colonial

An unusual-sounding name on Berkhamsted High Street is the Home and Colonial, an antiques emporium, with its name suggesting at a hint of its past history. Yet in the late nineteenth century, a draper's shop stood on the site of this very grand building. George Catherall was born in nearby Hemel Hempstead and had learned his trade in Slough, Berkshire. However, by the 1860s he had established his own draper's shop here in Berkhamsted. By 1881, George had increased his workforce to three assistants, of which one was his nephew and another his niece.

The *Bucks Herald* of February 1891 reported a somewhat unsavoury occurrence involving the Catheralls, which ended up in court:

> William Batchelor, Ann Batchelor, and Lillie Batchelor, all of Berkhampstead, were charged with assaulting Mr. George Catherall, of the same place, and George Catherall was charged with assaulting Ann Batchelor. Mr. Penny, [acting] for Mr. Catherall, stated that he was walking down High-street, Berkhampstead, and suddenly found himself assaulted from behind by two women, Lillie Batchelor and her mother, Ann Batchelor. The former was striking him with her fists, and the latter striking him over the head and shoulders with a stick. Directly afterwards William Batchelor (the husband) joined them in assaulting him [inside a shop]. Complainant shouted for the police, and P.C. Reed came and took defendant away.

A long-standing grievance was heightened by the defendant's (mistaken) belief that Catherall had sent offensive postcards to her. What a bizarre accusation to make. The *Bucks Herald* concluded its report: 'The Magistrates considered the case proved, and fined each of the Batchelors £1, including costs, which sums were paid, and they were bound over in £5 to keep the peace for six months. The summons against Mr. Catherall was dismissed.'

Catherall's Drapers is no longer in existence. By 1925, this High Street block was rebuilt as Home and Colonial Stores, one of the United Kingdom's largest retail chains at the time. It sold groceries and a range of 'colonial goods' including teas, coffees, spices, rice, sugar, chocolate and tobacco, all exotic wares imported from the colonies of the British Empire. After Home and Colonial closed, the

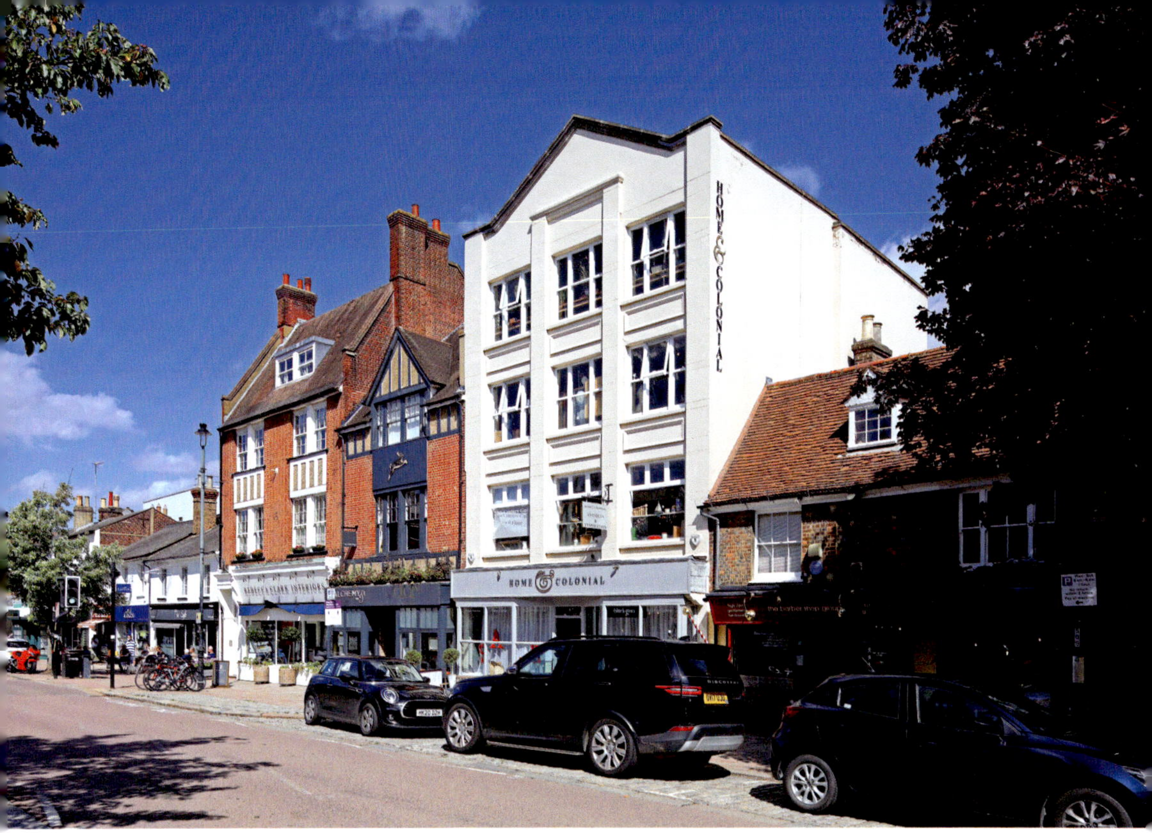

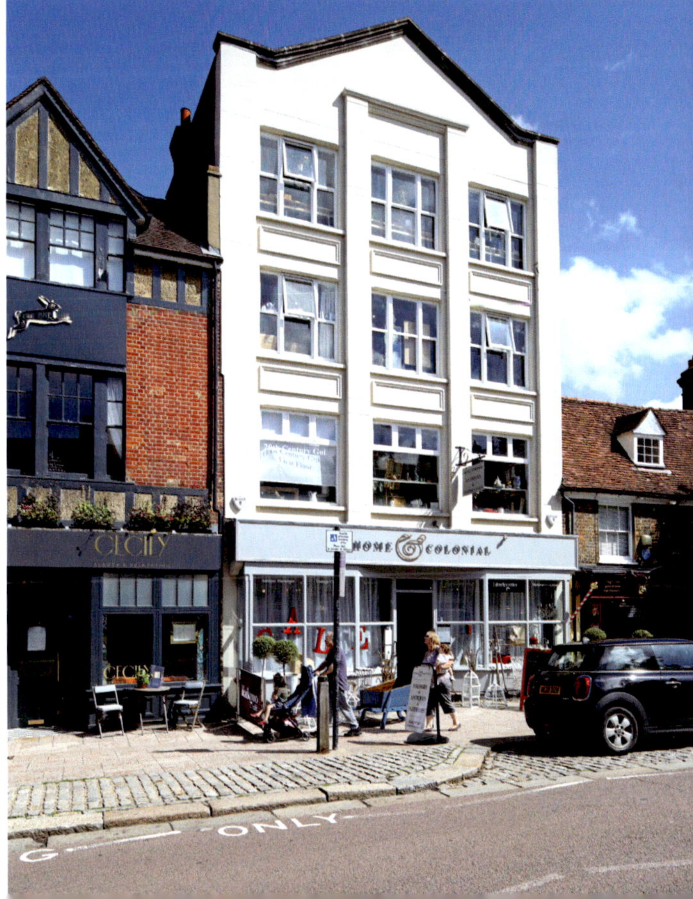

*Above and right*: The former residence of Home & Colonial, a standout building in the town.

four-storey building became Brandon's furniture store (later Neil's). Today it is a popular antiques shop, which has resurrected the classic Home and Colonial brand name.

## 45. Ashlyns School

Ashlyns dates back to the eighteenth century as a Foundling Hospital. A retired sea captain, Thomas Coram, became concerned about the number of unwanted children wandering the streets of London and infant bodies being abandoned on rubbish tips. He campaigned for a hospital to be built to accommodate and educate these children. In 1739, he was granted a royal charter to build the hospital, which was established at Lamb's Conduit Fields, Bloomsbury, in 1742 and was supported by many noted figures of the day in high society and the arts. Composer George Frederic Handel held benefit concerts in the Hospital Chapel to raise funds, performing his specially composed 'Foundling Hospital Anthem' and 'Messiah'.

In 1926, the hospital governors decided to relocate to a healthier, less polluted environment outside London. The children were relocated to Redhill, whilst the magnificent Georgian-style buildings here, based on the original hospital, were completed in 1935 to the designs of architect John Mortimer Sheppard. Many features from the original hospital can be found in the school and at the Coram Museum today. The organ, which had been personally donated to the Foundling Hospital by George Frederick Handel in the 1750s, was installed in the chapel (later moved to St Andrew's Holborn).

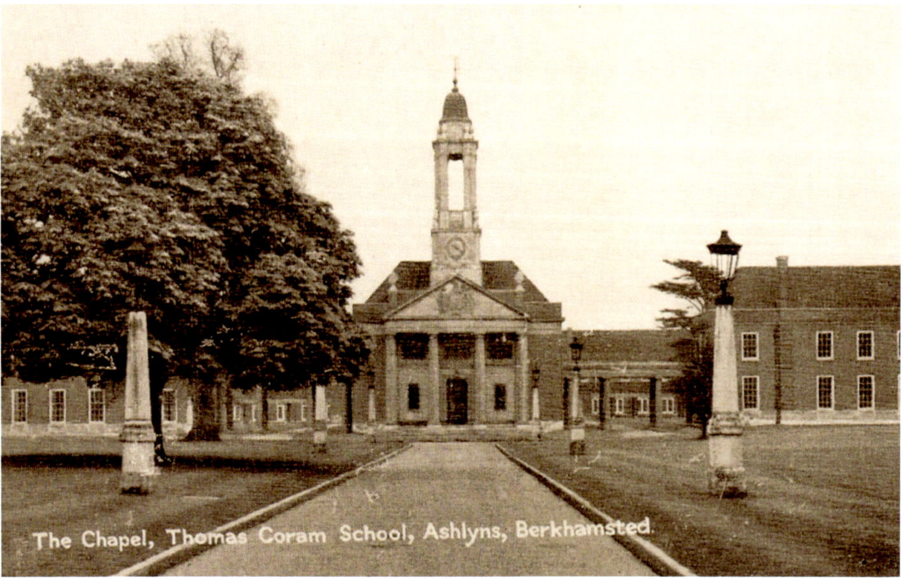


Ashlyns, once the Foundling Hospital.

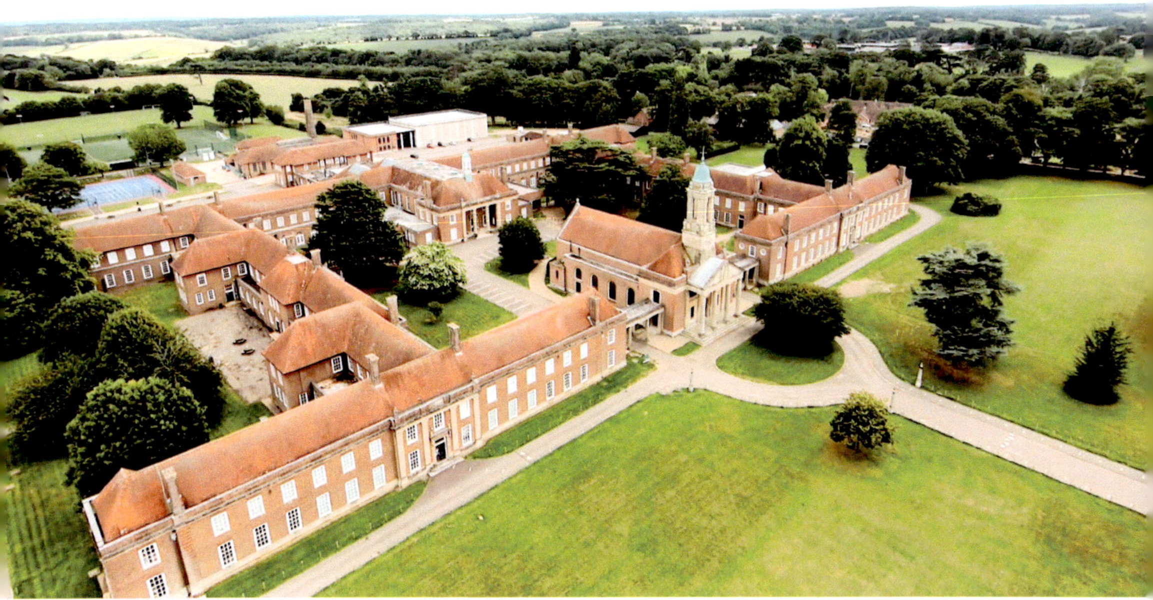

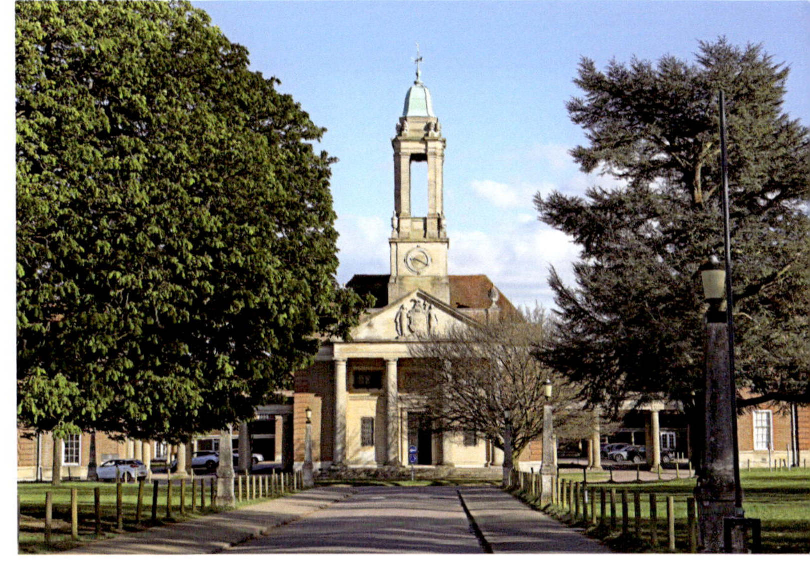

*Above*: Ashlyns is one of the finest buildings in Berkhamsted. (© Ashlyns School)

*Right*: The chapel was built to the designs of John Mortimer Sheppard. (© Ashlyns School)

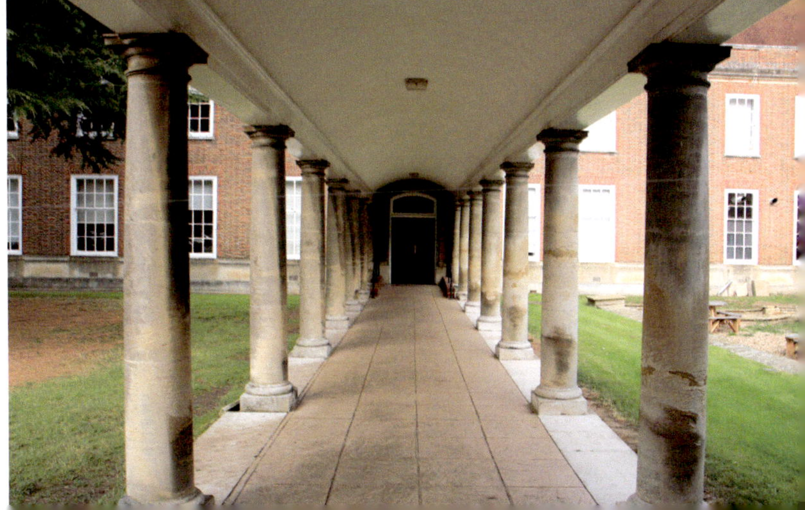

Georgian-style colonnades connecting many parts of the building.

In 1951, Hertfordshire County Council took responsibility for the educational element of the hospital, and it was renamed Ashlyns School. The Coram Foundation phased out boarders in 1955, when the foundation sold the buildings to the county council. The living accommodation was converted into classrooms and laboratories, and a 'grammar' stream was added to the school, making Ashlyns the first bilateral school in Hertfordshire.

By 1972, Ashlyns School had become a comprehensive upper school, forming part of the three-tier system of education which operated in Berkhamsted. The year 2013 heralded a new chapter in Ashlyns' history as they welcomed back students from the age of eleven to become a secondary school again.

The school is Grade II listed and has been the location for several film and award-winning television productions, including *The Crown*. The wealth of architectural features include the stained-glass windows in the chapel, the beautiful staircase in the entrance hall and the carved fireplace in the old board room.

Several books have also been inspired by the Foundling story, including *Lucky Button* by Michael Morpurgo, *Hetty Feather* by Jacqueline Wilson and *Coram Boy* by Jamila Gavin.

Historic England cite Ashlyns's School as having special interest as a fine Neo-Georgian-style school complex of 1932–35 by John Mortimer Sheppard, organised around a central courtyard with the chapel most prominent. It also has a very special historic interest for its associations with the famous 1745 Foundling Hospital in London, now demolished, but which was partly incorporated into the new school building.

## 46. The Rex and the Gatsby

The Rex and the Gatsby is one of the more unusual buildings in this Hertfordshire town. It was designed in the art deco style by architect David Evelyn Nye in 1936. It was opened as a cinema in 1938, but after half a century of service it closed in 1988 and became derelict. Following a campaign to save the Rex by a local entrepreneur, the cinema reopened to the public in 2004. It has a wonderful history.

In the 1930s, a cinema was already located on Berkhamsted High Street: the Court Cinema on the corner of Water Lane. It was acquired around 1930 by the Shipman & King cinema circuit, who also planned to open a second cinema in the town. They had originally intended to build on a site at the eastern end of town on the corner of Swing Gate Lane, but in 1936 S&K acquired Egerton House, a site closer to the centre of town which had spacious grounds for a cinema as well as a car park. Egerton House was demolished and the Rex was erected in its place. The cinema was opened on 9 May 1938 by Viscountess Davidson, and the first screening was the film *Heidi*, starring Shirley Temple.

By the 1970s, its popularity had waned and the Rex was no longer successful as a business. In January 1973, it was taken over by the Star Group, who renamed the cinema Studio 1. Films were shown Sunday to Wednesday, and Thursday to Sunday the building was given over to the more commercially lucrative pastime of bingo – like so many cinemas in this period. The dining room was filled with fruit machines. In 1976, the cinema changed hands once more and was taken over by the gambling company Zetters, who made major alterations to the building by dividing the auditorium into three sections. The last film to be shown on the big screen before this change was *Rollerball* on 7 April 1976. The circle was divided into two small studio screens, Studio 1 and Studio 2, while the stalls were converted to use as a full-time bingo hall. The studios opened on 11 April with *Swinging Wives* and *Sex in the Office* in Studio 1 and *The Bruce Lee Story* and *Somebody's Stolen our Russian Spy* in Studio 2.

Zetters' lease expired in 1988, and the Rex was sold to a property developer who planned to demolish the building to make way for new offices and flats. After a final screening of *The Witches of Eastwick* and *Teen Wolf Too*, the cinema closed its doors on 28 February 1988.

Efforts by campaigners resulted in the Rex being spot listed by English Heritage. A planning inspector for the Department of the Environment reported that Nye's building contributed to the 'diverse nature' of Berkhamsted High Street and that the quality and quantity of the surviving interior features merited preservation, and redevelopment plans were quashed. The building's listed status protected it from demolition and severely limited any redevelopment schemes. Various proposals were put forward for the site, including: a plan to convert the Rex auditorium into an atrium for an office building (1992); a proposal for an office complex with twin lecture theatres in the divided circle with a restored restaurant area (1993); and a plan to convert the building into a health spa (1997). These all failed to meet the strict criteria for a listed building, however. A fire in 1994 damaged the stage area. By this time the building had become very run down and the owners, Estates and General Property Company, attempted to have the building de-listed to enable demolition. In 1996, they attempted to dispose of the property and offered it to local entrepreneur James Hannaway for £450,000. Hannaway hoped to restore and reopen the cinema, but was unable to raise the money, and the Rex was bought by Nicholas King Homes.

A local campaign group, Friends of the Rex, was formed in 1997 with the aim of saving the Rex from demolition and acquiring it for use as a film centre, with film critic Barry Norman as their honorary president. The campaign was supported by the Twentieth Century Society, Joan Bakewell, and actors Hugh Grant, Hayley Mills and Ian Richardson. Campaigners formed the Rex Film and Arts Centre Trust to put forward a number of commercial proposals for a leisure complex including cinema screens, a swimming pool and a pub. The dilapidated state of the Rex was discussed in the House of Commons; Tom Clarke of the Department for Culture, Media and Sport declined to offer government subsidy for restoring the Rex, and local MP Richard Page took the view that the Rex was now an eyesore and should be de-listed and demolished to make way for sheltered housing.

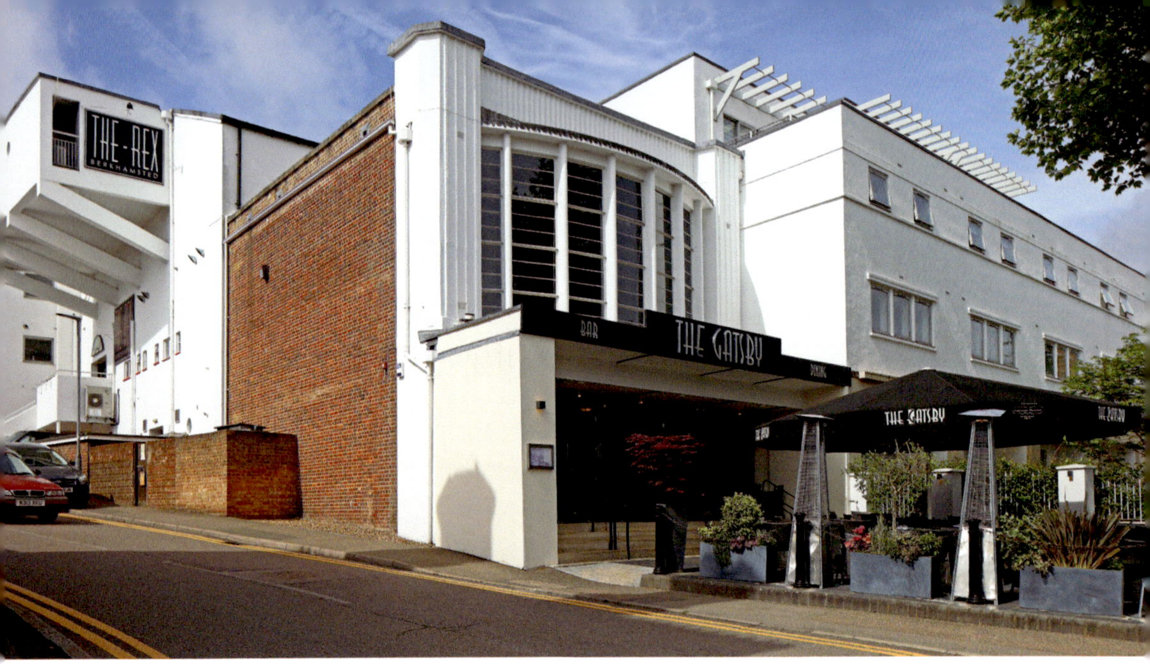

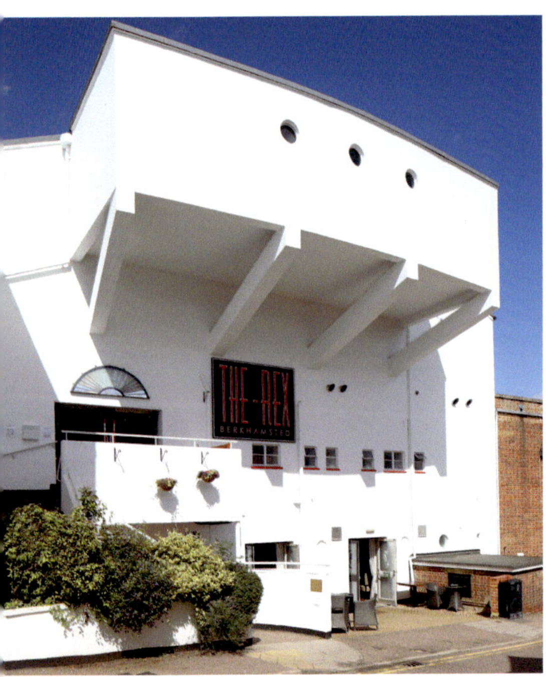

*Above*: The Rex and the Gatsby, now recognised as one of the finest art deco buildings in Hertfordshire.

*Left*: To maximise space, the projection booth was built into an exterior balcony protruding from the building above Three Close Lane, supported by large concrete brackets. It was accessed by an external iron staircase to reduce the fire risk of bringing flammable nitrate film reels into the theatre. A joke shared among local residents is that the architect had forgotten to add a projection room and that this box was added later.

The proposal from property developer Nicholas King Homes, which envisaged building an apartment block around the cinema (replacing the neighbouring shopfronts) and converting the Rex foyer into a bar and restaurant, was successful, and conversion of the site began in 2000.

The cinema reopened to the public in December 2004 with a screening of *The Third Man*, a film of particular significance as it was made during the heyday of the original Rex and the screenplay was by Berkhamsted writer Graham Greene.

The refurbishment was sympathetic to the cinema's art deco heritage, notably with the installation of a new chandelier and period-style mirrors. The work also brought about a major change to the building by separating the entire ground floor from the main cinema operation and converting it into a bar and restaurant. The decorated entrance foyer and dining room are now home to the Gatsby bar and restaurant, named in homage to the 1949 film *The Great Gatsby*, whose poster hangs above the bar, in front of the former cinema entrance at the top of the (now disused) staircase.

## 47. Berkhamsted Civic Centre

Berkhamsted Civic Centre is located on the High Street in the town centre and today accommodates the offices and meeting place of Berkhamsted Town Council.

In the nineteenth century, the main municipal building in the town was Berkhamsted Town Hall. After it was formed in 1898, Great Berkhampstead Urban District Council (as it was initially called) met in the local workhouse (on the corner of High Street and Kitsbury Road). In 1908, the council bought at auction the premises of a local building contractor, William Nash & Son, for the sum of £2,300. These premises comprised a house facing High Street, behind which was a former Wesleyan Chapel (by then used as a workshop), with a large yard and other outbuildings. These premises were converted to serve as the council's offices and meeting place, with the former chapel becoming the council chamber. In the early 1930s, after the council decided it needed more office space, it acquired the adjacent fishmonger's shop and demolished both buildings. The new Civic Centre was designed by the council surveyor, John Hadfield, in the Neo-Georgian style, built in red brick with stone dressings and was officially opened by the chairman of the council, Councillor Walter Pitkin, on 14 October 1938.

The design involved a symmetrical main frontage with seven bays facing onto the High Street; the central bay, which slightly projected forward, featured a round-headed entrance with brick voussoirs, a keystone, wrought-iron gates and a deeply recessed doorway inside. There was a wrought-iron balconet and French door on the first floor, flanked by pilasters supporting an open pediment, while the other bays were fenestrated by sash windows on both floors. Internally, the principal rooms were a courtroom on the ground floor and a council meeting room on the first floor.

The council maintained garaging behind the Civic Centre for the local fire engines until 1969, when the fire service moved to Castle Street. The Civic Centre continued to serve as the local seat of government until the enlarged Dacorum Borough Council was formed in 1974. The courtroom was subsequently converted into an assembly hall, and the council meeting room became the offices and meeting place of Berkhamsted Town Council. In the 1980s and 1990s, the Civic Centre was a significant events venue. The rock band Marillion performed their first concert there in 1980, the jazz singer Elaine Delmar performed there in 1986, and the American jazz tenor saxophonist Scott Hamilton took part in a BBC concert, which was broadcast from there in 1998. Also, the Master of the Queen's Music, Malcolm Williamson, delivered at least one premiere of his works at the Civic Centre in the 1980s.

A wooden sign bearing the coat of arms of the town was presented by the Berkhamsted Citizens Association and erected on the pavement outside the Civic Centre in 1983. The garaging behind the Civic Centre, previously used by the fire service, was converted into a museum store for Dacorum Heritage in 1994.

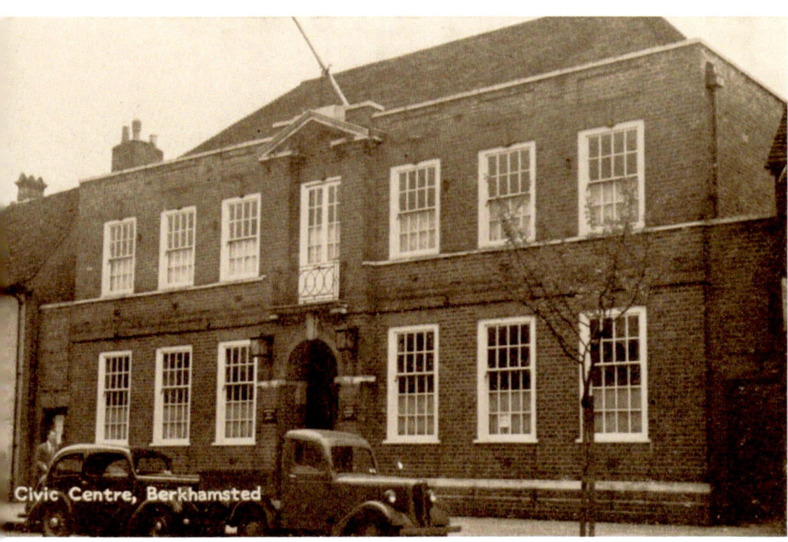


*Left*: An early view of the Civic Centre.

*Below*: A symmetrical façade of the town's centre of government.

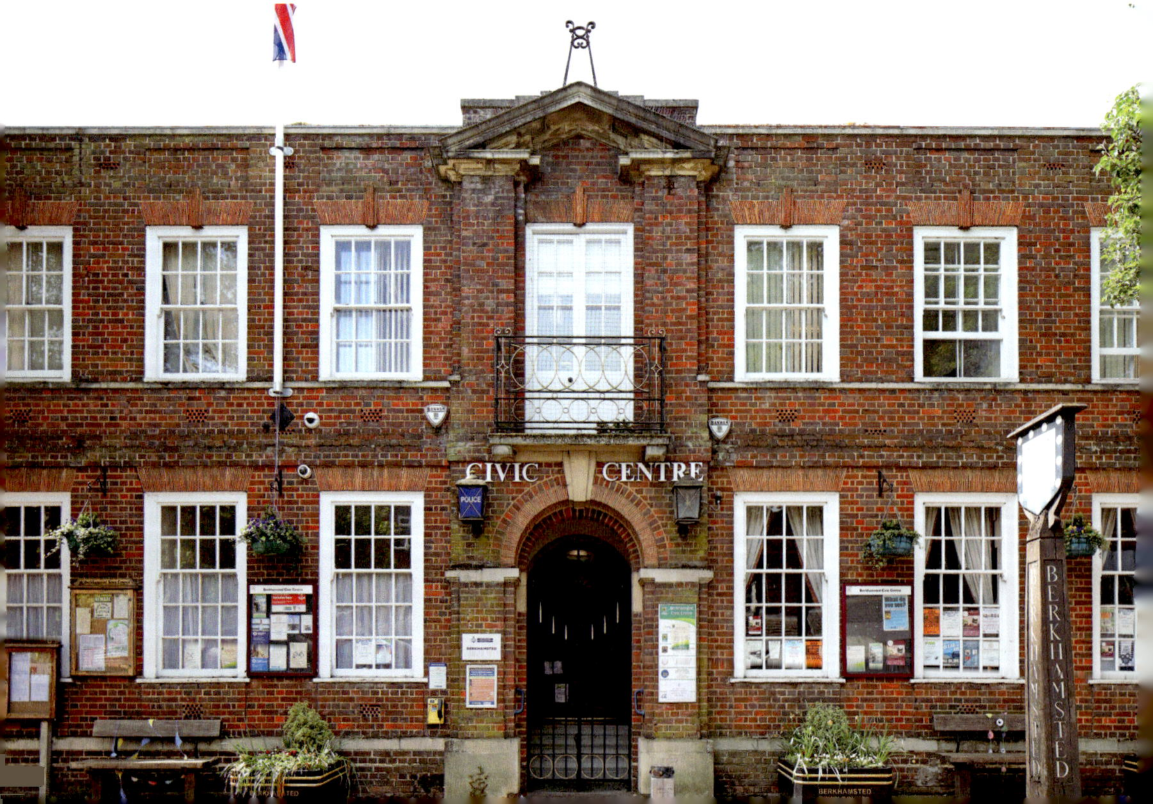

## 48. Former DeLisle Jewellers

Just as pawnbrokers signal their presence with three suspended balls, and barbers have their red-and-white striped poles, so jewellers, clockmakers and watchmakers have traditionally attracted attention with elaborate projecting clocks, turret clocks or time balls. Examples can be found on high streets throughout the country.

Some jewellers were particularly ambitious with their public timepieces, seeking to outdo the local competition. They wanted something eye-catching and novel. Some jewellers preferred a turret clock – perhaps more visible from a distance, though not easily viewed by window shoppers. A turret clock and cupola over a modest mid-twentieth-century parade of shops on the corner of High Street and Lower Kings Road, here in Berkhamsted, bears the name of the former local

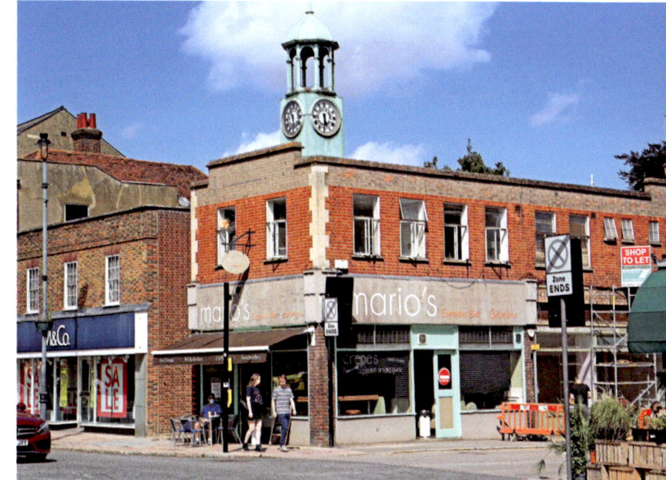

*Right*: The former De Lisle & Sons business and its turret clock.

*Below*: An excellent example of raising the head slightly and an architectural feature unique to the town.

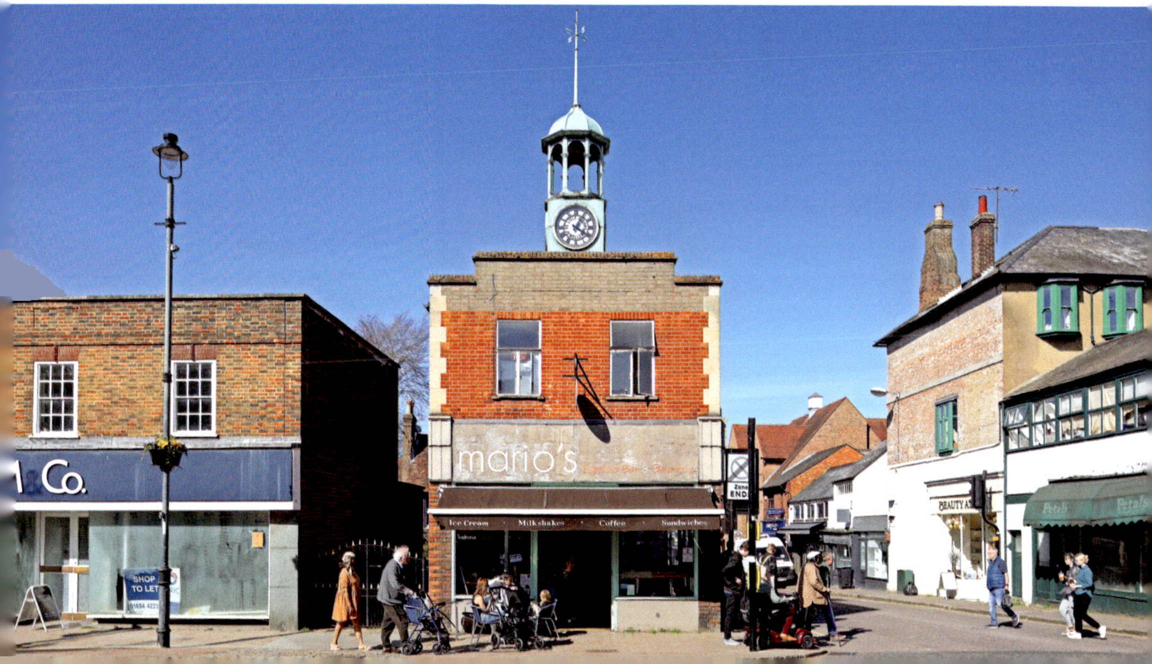

watchmaker, jeweller and clockmaker E. C. De Lisle & Sons. Like most of the clocks of the era, it has Roman rather than Arabic numerals.

Prior uses of the building included Edward Henry Morris & Sons, who were watch and clockmakers as well as a tobacconist, a bookshop, and fishmonger.

## 49. Site of Former Counting House

Little remains of William Cooper's chemical works in Berkhamsted today (see building Nos 21 and 25). The majority of the buildings have been demolished and replaced with flats, but evidence still exists in the town. Cooper House on Ravens Lane, now an apartment block, was originally the administration building for Cooper's and the name is visible above the front door. On the opposite side of the road, the Clunbury Court apartment building that was built in 2002 bears the inscription 'Site of former counting house', marking the location of Cooper's accounts department. The company name is also remembered in the nearby street names of Cooper Way, Robertson Road and McDougall Road. Although the industry is long gone, the names of the people who helped Berkhamsted to flourish are never forgotten.

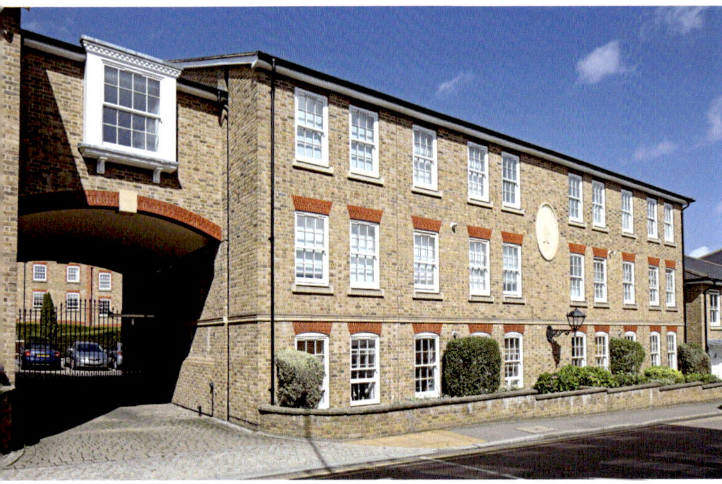

The site of the former counting house of William Cooper's chemical works.

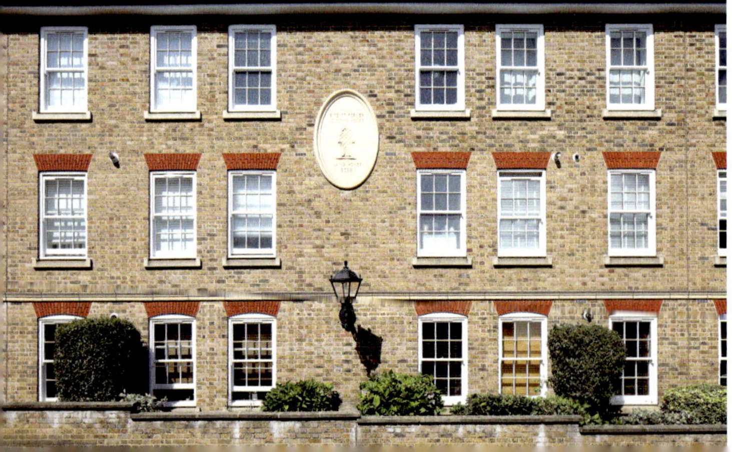

Local history commemorated in this modern building.

## 50. Modern Berkhamsted

Today, Berkhamsted is a viable and prosperous provincial market town in Hertfordshire and comes under the governance of Dacorum Borough Council. As set out in the council's Town Centre Strategy for the town, the council's aim 'is to conserve and enhance the town centre environment with particular reference to retention of its appearance, character and atmosphere as a small county town centre … [and] to address the problems of the 1990s post-bypass era'.

Berkhamsted, like many small county towns, is inevitably subject to pressures. Pressures exist for commercial and retail infrastructure development that is in conflict with, and can be out of scale with, the town centre's environmental quality, in particular its small country town character.

However, recent large-scale residential developments have been built both within and on the edge of the town centre conservation area; flats, terraces and semi-detached houses on former commercial or industrial sites. The increase in population will bring added pressures for greater amenities and the need for improvements to the existing infrastructure.

Royal Quays, described as an 'attractive collection of 54 private apartments and houses set in grounds extending to approximately 4.8 acres. There are areas of the gardens at Royal Keys that have been designed for the use and enjoyment "of all the residents" – a quiet place to sit or gently stroll along the River Bulbourne – or simply look upon them as landscaped open space that allows the development to breathe.'

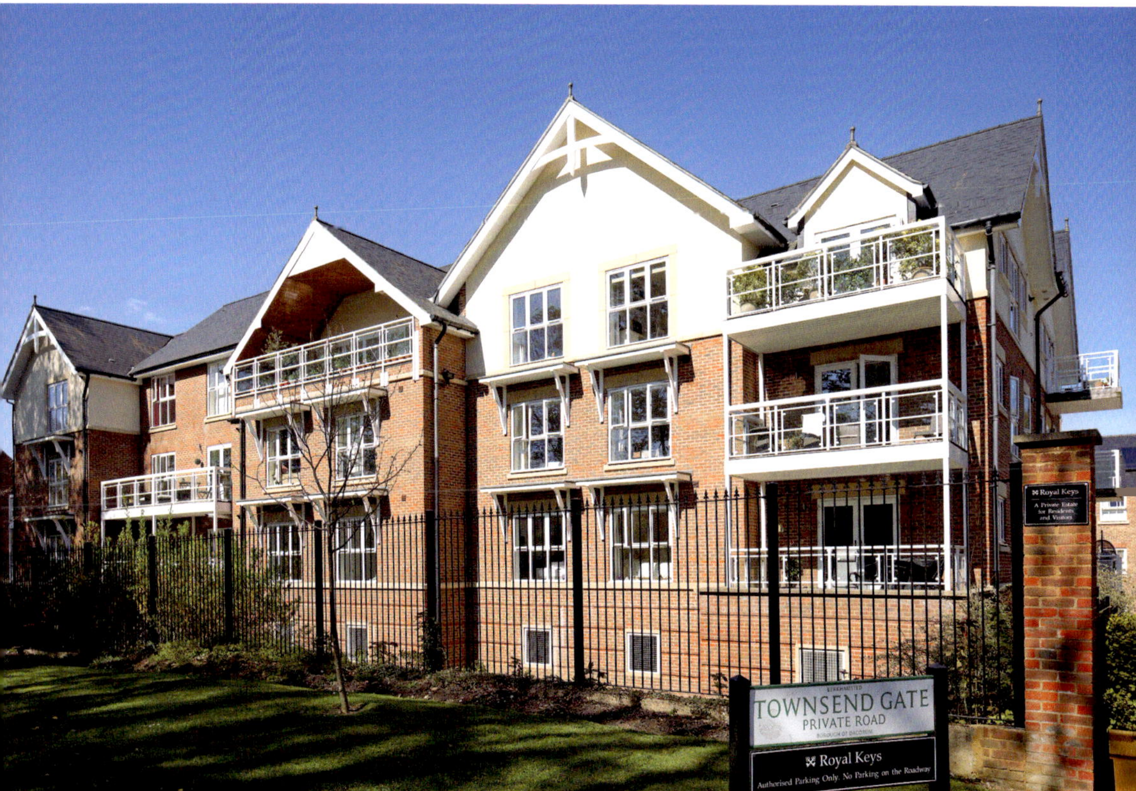

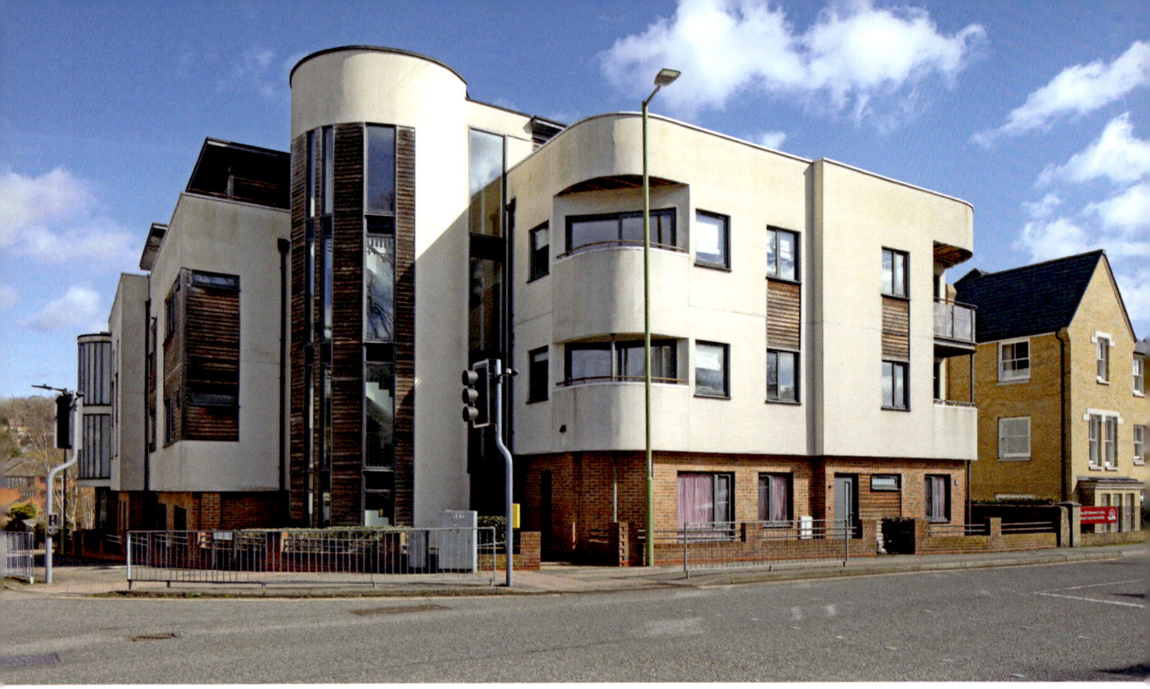

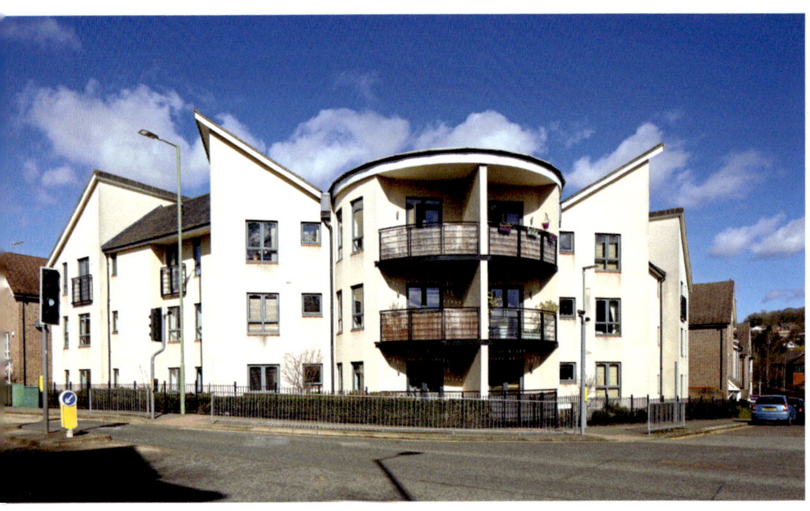

Dell Court, Northchurch.

Quennell House, Sheldon Way, modern apartments. Charles and Majorie Quennell came to Berkhamsted in 1917. At their home in Shrublands Road they wrote and illustrated the first volume of a popular series of books entitled *A History of Everyday Things in England*. Charles was also an architect and designed the Berkhamsted war memorial.

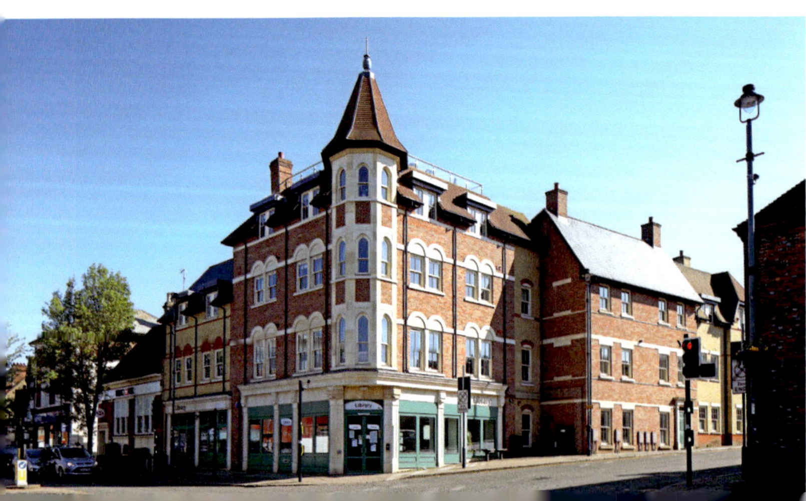

The county library.

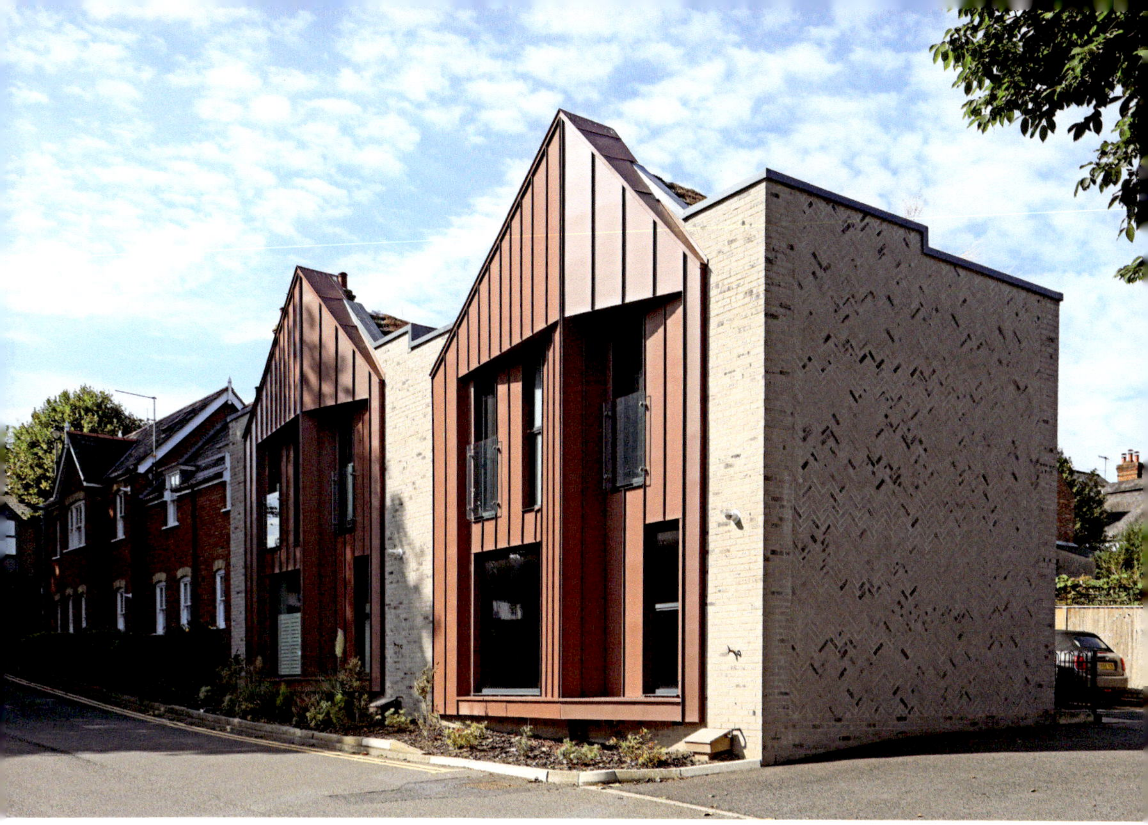

*Above*: Modern houses – very different to others in the town centre's conservation area.

*Below*: Waitrose supermarket lies behind Lower Kings Road and the High Street, on back land next to the River Bulbourne, and occupies the site of the former Bulbourne (clothing) factory.

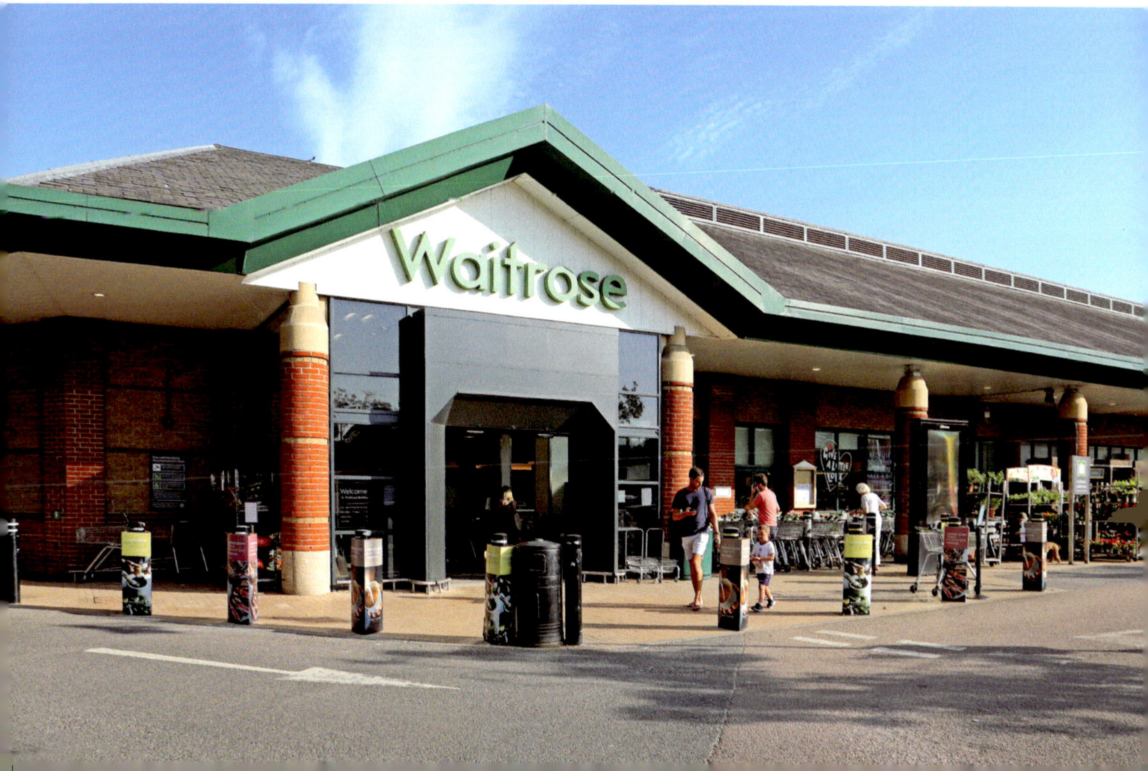

# Bibliography


Berkhamsted Local History & Museum Society, *Berkhamsted Through Time* (Amberley Publishing: Stroud, 2013)

Birtchnell, Percy, C., *Bygone Berkhamsted* (White Crescent Press Ltd, 1975)

Birtchnell, Percy, C., *A Short History of Berkhamsted* (1972)

Cobb, J., *History and Antiquities of Berkhamsted* (The Bookstack: Berkhamsted, 1988)

Cook, John, *Berkhamsted's Story: A Book for the Millennium* (Berkhamsted Town Council, 1999)

Hastie, Scott, *Berkhamsted: An Illustrated History* (Alpine Press: Kings Langley, 1999)

Hemel Hempstead Gazette, *Hemel Hempstead, Berkhamsted and Tring: A Century of Change* (Breedon Books Publishing Co. Ltd, 2002)

Meadows, Eric, G., *Berkhamsted: A Gateway to The Chilterns* (The Bookstack: Berkhamsted, 2001)

Nash, H., *Reminiscences of Berkhamsted* (The Bookstack: Berkhamsted, 1988)

# Acknowledgements

**Paul Rabbitts** would like to thank Peter Jeffree for once again capturing the wonderful buildings in this very fine Hertfordshire town. My thanks to the many coffee shops and bookshops in the town. I love browsing within them and partaking in numerous lattes and ginger biscuits on my many forays from the other side of the border of Central Bedfordshire.

I would like to acknowledge the considerable research undertaken by those associated with the Rectory Lane Cemetery (see rectorylanecemetery.org.uk). Much of the information within this book has been researched from their fabulous website, which was funded by the Heritage Fund and Community Fund. Many of the individuals referred to in this history are also buried in Rectory Lane Cemetery. It is well worth a visit. Also, do pay a visit to the work undertaken by the Berkhamsted Local History & Museum Society (see berkhamsted-history.org.uk).

**Peter Jeffree** would like to thank Paul Rabbitts for his excellent research and text, which brings to life the backstory of Berkhamsted's many historic buildings. He would also like to thank his wife, who has tolerated many trips to Berkhamsted to capture images of the town's significant buildings at different times of day. He would echo Paul's praise for the many and varied café's in Berkhamsted which provide an extra incentive to visit the town centre.

# About the Authors

**Dr Paul Rabbitts** is a Fellow of the Royal Society of Arts, as well as a Fellow of the Royal Historical Society. He has managed public parks, culture and heritage for thirty-five years for various local authorities from Carlisle, Middlesbrough, Watford, Southend-on-Sea and Norwich. He is also a prolific author on architecture, public parks and a noted expert on the history of public parks as well as the Victorian and Edwardian bandstand. He has written several books in Amberley's '50 Buildings' series, including Watford (with Peter), Leighton Buzzard, Aylesbury, Luton, Salford, Bournemouth, Windsor, Carlisle, Salisbury, Welwyn and Welwyn Garden City (with Peter), Hertford (with Peter), Tring, Dunstable and Manchester. He currently lives in Leighton Buzzard.

**Peter Jeffree** is a retired architect and lifelong photography enthusiast, who dedicates his time to capturing images of modern and historic buildings in the UK and abroad. He has contributed photos to several books in this series authored by Paul Rabbitts. Peter has lived in Watford for forty-five years.